I0430156

REVISING
FOR
EFFECT

Key Concepts

that will help you

to improve your writing

SUZANNE R. ROY

Copyright © 2014 Suzanne R. Roy

All rights reserved.

ISBN: 1500184608
ISBN-13: 978-1500184605

ACKNOWLEDGMENT

As I put the finishing touches on this book about Key Concepts in revision, I recognize that I owe special thanks to my oldest brother, Roland M. Roy, for helping me to refine these concepts many years ago when we offered business writing seminars together, and for his recent assistance in fine-tuning and proofing this text. Since he still teaches the concepts in his classes at the University of Maine in Augusta, his feedback has been invaluable.

CONTENTS

INTRODUCTION

Whenever I'm asked by my clients to revise a letter or other written communication for them, I'm always amazed at how easy it is to improve the text simply by determining the approach that should have been taken, given the subject and purpose of the message being conveyed, and by applying one or more of the Key Concepts that will be explained in this book. It amazes me even more to see how few people are aware of how quickly they could enhance their writing simply by taking a few minutes to revise their work for effect.

 The approach and the concepts presented in this book were developed years ago when I was teaching English at the University of Maine, and they were refined, with the help of my brother Roland M. Roy, when he and I conducted writing seminars for businesses in our area. The approach is not complicated, and the concepts are so simple to understand and seem so obvious that you may wonder why they need to be taught at all. However, as I'm sure you've discovered through the years, it's often the simplest and most obvious things that we overlook when searching for ways to improve our lives and, in this case, our writing. Once you've gone through each chapter and learned how to apply the concepts to your writing, you'll see how quickly you can enhance your written communication to make it more effective.

The Key Concepts approach

Throughout this book, you will be asked to use a 5-step process in order to determine how and where to apply each of the Key Concepts. This method of re-"vising" – i.e., re-"viewing" – your work will help you to develop the habit of focusing on the subject and purpose of your message and will help you to see more clearly how and where you can change your message to have the greatest effect on your reader.

Before we begin, however, there are two directives that you will encounter throughout the book that I'd like to be sure you understand:

The first directive is "scan."

◉ By "scan," I mean that you should simply give the example under study a quick look to see what strikes you or what stands out that relates to the Key Concept under discussion. This step should take you only a few seconds and is meant to:

▸ give you a sense of how most readers will approach what you've written and form their initial impressions of your message, and

▸ help you to understand more clearly the nature and purpose of the Key Concept you are learning about.

The second directive is "analyze."

By "analyze," I mean that you should read the example with the goals of identifying the subject and purpose of the message and of listing the elements in the text that are related to the Key Concept being studied. This will allow you to see how the Key Concept can be applied.

A word of caution about the Writing Process

It's important that you remember that the writing process involves six steps: generating ideas, organizing them, writing a draft, stepping away from the draft, revising it, and editing it. This text obviously deals with the fifth step in the process: revision.

If the concepts discussed in this book are to be of any value to you as a writer, they must be applied to your writing only AFTER you have committed your words to paper. To attempt to revise your writing while you're still in the drafting stage is not only foolish but counter-productive and may actually interfere with the creative process. If you focus your energy on the task of getting your ideas down on paper during the first stages of the writing process and then allow yourself at least a small amount of time away from that first draft, you will then be free to apply what you've learned in this text to the written words you have in front of you, and you'll discover that revising can be both fascinating and rewarding. Furthermore, once you've become adept at revising, you'll need to do less of it because you'll incorporate during the drafting stage much of what you've learned in this book without being consciously focused on doing so.

My challenge to you

My brother still teaches these concepts in his University Communication classes, and I use them all the time in my work as a business consultant. They are time-tested and they work, so if you're serious about improving your writing, I challenge you to jump in and become familiar with the contents of this book. You'll be happy you did.

KEY CONCEPT #1: EMPHASIS

Introduction

How do you emphasize words or ideas that you think are important or that you want your audience to pay particular attention to?

In speech, you probably repeat those words or ideas, stress them through tone of voice, or even shout them out to be sure they are heard. However, what do you do to create emphasis in writing?

Some writers underline what they want to stress, while others use capitals to call attention to important words. In fact, there are many ways to create emphasis in writing, some of them so simple to use that a writer may use them without realizing their effect.

In order to communicate effectively, you must understand emphasis techniques so that you can emphasize what is most important in your message and de-emphasize what will detract from or weaken that message.

Emphasis is a Key Concept because of several factors:

Different readers will approach your writing from different perspectives.

- Emphasis helps to focus your reader on <u>your</u> perspective.

Most readers will be bombarded with so many ideas in the course of the day that they will need help in prioritizing them.

- Emphasis shows your reader how <u>you</u> want your ideas prioritized.

Most readers are likely to scan most reading materials they receive.

- Emphasis assures that your most important ideas and messages will stand out even when scanned.

Emphasis is a very simple concept to understand and a simple one to control. It's also easy to spot because, to a large extent, emphasis techniques are *scannable* -- that is, they can be spotted simply by scanning quickly through written text.

Emphasis techniques are based largely on common sense but are often overlooked precisely because they seem so obvious. As you study these techniques, you may be surprised to discover how often people emphasize ideas they don't want emphasized in their writing and fail to emphasize ideas they consider very important, simply because they don't recognize the concept. Don't make these types of errors. They can be costly.

Types of emphasis in writing

In writing, there are <u>three</u> types of emphasis to consider: *physical*, *grammatical*, and *psychological*. In analyzing each type of emphasis, look at all techniques – both positive and negative – separately and objectively since they can all be applied to written material to affect emphasis.

Creating Physical Emphasis

Physical emphasis involves the visible presentation or layout of ideas. Here are ways in which you can physically <u>emphasize</u> a written idea:

- Use headings or subject lines to signal it.
- Print it in a different font, color, typestyle, or character (e.g., numbers will stand out when surrounded by lettered text).
- Underline it or write it in bold or in caps.
- Indent it.
- List it or point to it with bullets.

- Put it within quotation marks or parentheses or between dashes.

- Set it apart from other text (e.g., in its own paragraph).

These methods will work if they are not overused and if they differ from the surrounding text.

Conversely, here's how you can physically <u>deemphasize</u> a written idea:

- Do not place it in headings or subject lines.

- Present it in normal point size, font, color, typestyle, or character.

- Do not underline it or write it in bold or in caps.

- Do not list it or point to it with bullets.

- Do not indent it.

- Do not use special punctuation with it.

- Do not set it apart from other text.

These methods of de-emphasizing ideas will work if they allow the targeted ideas to blend in with the physical appearance of the words that surround them.

<u>To revise your writing for physical emphasis, I recommend the following 5-step revision process</u>:

Step 1: **<u>Scan</u>** the text (remember: the scanning should take you no more than a second or two) **and list** what has been physically emphasized – i.e., what stands out visually – in the message.

Step 2: <u>Analyze</u> the message more closely to determine its subject and purpose **and list** the key ideas that explain or support that purpose.

Step 3: <u>Compare</u> the two lists to determine what should have been emphasized and, if applicable, what should have been de-emphasized in the message.

Step 4: <u>Plan</u> the revision based what you've discovered by comparing the two lists.

Step 5: <u>Revise</u> the text.

[NOTE: This same basic process will be applied in dealing with each of the Key Concepts explained in this book.]

<u>Now, let's apply the process to discover how emphasis is used in the following example:</u>

SUBJECT:

I HAVE A CUSTOMER WHO IS MOVING SEPTEMBER 4TH. <u>SHE IS INTERESTED IN SELLING A TALL CHEST WITH DRAWERS</u> PURCHASED 4 YEARS AGO. THE TCDR CURRENTLY SELLS FOR $4475. THE 2010 PIECE CAN BE OFFERED FOR SALE FOR <u>$4000</u>. IF YOU HAVE ANYONE INTERESTED IN THIS PIECE, PLEASE CONTACT ME OR HAVE THE POTENTIAL BUYER CONTACT ME. THANKS FOR YOUR HELP. THIS IS AN EXCELLENT CUSTOMER SO I THINK IT WILL BENEFIT US IN THE FUTURE.

Step 1: Here's what your 1st list – i.e., your list of what stands out visually in the text – should look like:

- 👁 The label "*SUBJECT*" because of its unique position
- 👁 The numbers that identify how long ago the piece was purchased, the year the piece was made, and the price figures
- 👁 "*SHE IS INTERESTED IN SELLING A TALL CHEST WITH DRAWERS*" and "*$4000*" because these items have been underlined.

Step 2: The subject of the message is that an item is being put up for sale by a valued customer, and the purpose is to enlist the reader's help in selling the item. If you analyze the message more closely, your list of key ideas that must be conveyed to the reader in order to make the message effective should include the following:

- 👁 The announcement of the sale
- 👁 The importance of the customer
- 👁 The specifics relating to the age of the piece and the price figures
- 👁 The request for action
- 👁 The thank you for help received or anticipated

Step 3: If you compare the two lists, here's what you'll discover was not emphasized in the message:

- ➢ The importance of the customer
- ➢ The request for assistance in selling the item
- ➢ The "thank you" for help received or anticipated

I hope you also noticed the following:

- ➤ The empty subject line was a missed opportunity to highlight the subject and/or purpose of the message.

- ➤ The fact that the message was written entirely in capital letters made the message difficult to scan. Not only did the overuse of capitals render that particular emphasis technique useless, but it made the text more difficult to read because there were no typographical variations in the letters to assist the reader in quickly scanning the material. All caps could also be seen by some readers as shouting and, thus, weaken the message or alienate the reader.

- ➤ Information relating to how long ago the piece was purchased was emphasized unnecessarily.

Step 4: Your plan to revise the text using physical emphasis techniques might look like this:

- ☑ First, use normal type to make the message more readable and to allow for more effective use of other emphasis techniques.

- ☑ Next, consider listing the price figures to help keep the message simple and easy to read.

- ☑ Set the request and thank you apart from the rest of the text.

- ☑ Finally, emphasize the controlling idea by referring to it in the subject line.

Step 5: Based on your plan, see how the revision compares to the original:

<u>Original version</u>

SUBJECT:

I HAVE A CUSTOMER WHO IS MOVING SEPTEMBER 4TH. <u>SHE IS INTERESTED IN SELLING A TALL CHEST WITH DRAWERS</u> PURCHASED 4 YEARS AGO. THE TCDR CURRENTLY SELLS FOR $4475. THE 2010 PIECE CAN BE OFFERED FOR SALE FOR <u>$4000</u>. IF YOU HAVE ANYONE INTERESTED IN THIS PIECE, PLEASE CONTACT ME OR HAVE THE POTENTIAL BUYER CONTACT ME. THANKS FOR YOUR HELP. THIS IS AN EXCELLENT CUSTOMER SO I THINK IT WILL BENEFIT US IN THE FUTURE.

<u>Revised version</u>

SUBJECT: Special request on behalf of valued customer

One of our valued customers, who is moving September 4th, is interested in selling a tall chest with drawers (TCDR) originally purchased four years ago.

- *Current price for a new TCDR = $4475*
- *Asking price for this 2010 piece = $4000*

If you have anyone interested in this piece, please contact me or have the potential buyer contact me.

Thanks for your help. This is an excellent customer, so I think our efforts will benefit us in the future.

<u>Please notice the following</u>:

- ✪ The subject line, which is highlighted in bold, identifies the purpose of the message and mentions the customer's importance.

- ✪ Underlining was not necessary because the sale item is not deeply buried in this message.

- ✪ The item and its cost are emphasized both by the bulleted list and by the use of numbers.

- ✪ The number of years since the purchase ("4"), on the other hand, is written out because it does not deserve the emphasis that the other numbers do and could actually distract the reader from the important information.

- ✪ The request and the thank you have been placed in their own paragraphs to separate them from the rest of the text.

This message has obviously been improved and made easier to read simply through the use of physical emphasis techniques.

Creating Grammatical Emphasis

Grammatical emphasis refers to the emphasis you create by means of clause construction, subordination, sentence structure, and style. Writers who don't have a clear understanding of grammar often make mistakes in this area without realizing it. Any writer who works to understand how language functions has an edge in controlling emphasis and in creating truly effective written communications.

You <u>emphasize</u> an idea grammatically when you do the following:

- Make it the subject of your independent clauses.
- Express it in simple sentences.
- Maintain focus on it by varying your style.

You <u>deemphasize</u> an idea grammatically when you do the following:

- Present it primarily in dependent (subordinate) clauses.
- Present it in compound sentences.
- Shift the focus to other ideas.

[Note: If you cannot recognize clauses, you may want to refer to the first book in this series: "*Understanding CLAUSE AND EFFECT*," which is available in both print and eBook form.]

<u>To revise your writing for grammatical emphasis, follow this 5-step revision process</u>:

Step 1: <u>Scan</u> the message <u>**and list**</u> the independent clauses in the message to see what has been grammatically emphasized.

Step 2: <u>Analyze</u> the message more closely to determine its subject and purpose <u>**and list**</u> all the key points that need to be conveyed to make the message effective.

Step 3: <u>Compare</u> the two lists to determine what should have been emphasized and, if applicable, what should have been de-emphasized in the message.

Step 4: <u>Plan</u> the revision based on what you've discovered in comparing the two lists.

Step 5: <u>Revise</u> the text.

<u>Let's apply our revision process to spot how grammatical emphasis has been or should have been used in the following example</u>:

> *RE: Documentation of credentials*
>
> *Our licensing and accrediting agencies have determined that we do not have sufficient evidence to prove that you are qualified to do your job. Therefore, it becomes necessary for us to obtain documentation from you which indicates that you have indeed successfully completed the educational level which you indicated on your initial employment application form with this agency. Would you please furnish a copy of your high school diploma or graduate equivalency diploma, college diploma or transcripts, and/or any other pertinent information to your immediate supervisor by April 30. If you anticipate any difficulty in their acquisition, it is imperative that you contact your immediate supervisor as soon as possible since continuation of employment may be contingent on it.*

Step #1: Your list of the the independent clauses in the message should include the following:

- 👁 *"Our licensing and accrediting agencies have determined"*

- 👁 *"Therefore, it becomes necessary for us to obtain documentation from you"*

- 👁 *"Would you please furnish a copy of your high school diploma or graduate equivalency diploma, college diploma or transcripts, and/or any other pertinent information to your immediate supervisor by April 30."*

- 👁 *"...it is imperative"*

Step #2:   The subject of the message is the employer's need for additional background documentation, and the purpose is to alert "you" – the employee – to the need to provide that documentation as soon as possible to avoid problems. Your list of key points should include the following:

- The absence of proof that you qualify for the job

- The need to provide specific documentation of your educational qualifications to your supervisor by April 30th

- The need to let your supervisor know of any delays

- The potential consequences of not providing the information as soon as possible

Step #3: Comparison of the two lists:

- ➢ The need to provide specific documentation by the deadline has been emphasized by being expressed in an independent clause.

> ➤ The other key points have been deemphasized by being expressed in dependent clauses.

To help you see more clearly what's been de-emphasized, here are a few of the dependent clauses in the message:

> ▸ *that we do not have sufficient evidence to prove that you are qualified to do your job* (2 dependent clauses)

> ▸ *If you anticipate any difficulty in their acquisition*

> ▸ *that you contact your immediate supervisor as soon as possible*

> ▸ *since continuation of employment may be contingent on it*

Step #4: At this point, it should have become clear that the message deals with important directives that the reader must understand and comply with immediately. Yet, the directives are in danger of being overlooked by the reader because some of the most important ideas (including the clauses that focus on the reader) have been deemphasized, and the main focus has been placed primarily on the writer. As a result, the message is wordy and weak.

> ☑ You'll have to restructure the clauses to be sure the key ideas are not subordinated but stand out as the main ideas expressed in each sentence.

This restructuring should improve the focus as well.

Step #5: Here is a preliminary revision. I've underlined the independent clauses so that you can compare them to the list you made in Step 1:

> *RE: Urgent request for documentation of job credentials*
>
> *According to our licensing and accrediting agencies, <u>we do not have sufficient evidence to prove</u> that you are qualified to do your job. To remain employed with us, <u>you must provide us with documentation to prove</u> that you have successfully completed the educational level you indicated on your initial employment application form with this agency. <u>Please furnish a copy of your high school diploma or graduate equivalency diploma, college diploma or transcripts, and/or any other pertinent information to your immediate supervisor by April 30</u>. If you anticipate any difficulty in collecting this information, <u>contact your immediate supervisor as soon as possible</u> since continuation of employment may be contingent on it.*

As you can see, the strongest ideas are expressed in independent clauses. Also, the focus remains on the reader after the initial statement is made, especially with the use of direct requests (*Please, contact*) in which the subject *"you"* is understood.

Now, let's apply the physical emphasis techniques we discussed earlier to make the message more effective.

Original version

RE: Documentation of credentials

Our licensing and accrediting agencies have determined that we do not have sufficient evidence to prove that you are qualified to do your job. Therefore, it becomes necessary for us to obtain documentation from you which indicates that you have indeed successfully completed the educational level which you indicated on your initial employment application form with this agency. Would you please furnish a copy of your high school diploma or graduate equivalency diploma, college diploma or transcripts, and/or any other pertinent information to your immediate supervisor by April 30. If you anticipate any difficulty in their acquisition, it is imperative that you contact your immediate supervisor as soon as possible since continuation of employment may be contingent on it.

Revised version

RE: Urgent request for documentation of job credentials

According to our licensing and accrediting agencies, we do not have sufficient evidence to prove that you are qualified to do your job.

To remain employed with us, you must provide us with documentation to prove that you have successfully completed the educational level you indicated on your initial employment application form with this agency.

Please furnish the following information to your immediate supervisor by April 30th:

- *A copy of your high school diploma or graduate equivalency diploma, college diploma, or college transcripts, as applicable, and*
- *Any other pertinent information that relates to your job qualifications.*

If you anticipate any difficulty in collecting this information, contact your immediate supervisor as soon as possible since continuation of employment may be contingent on it.

As you can see, you've already learned some very useful tools for making your written communications more effective. As you may have noted, now that the letter is more well organized, you could probably find ways to make it even more forceful and more concise.

Creating Psychological Emphasis

Psychological emphasis refers to the emphasis you create in the mind of the reader. In other words, you can emphasize ideas not only through your choice of physical layout and grammatical construction but also by controlling the associations and images the reader links to those ideas.

You <u>emphasize</u> your subject psychologically when you do the following:

- Present your subject first or last in a particular body of text (i.e., a sentence, a paragraph, a section, a chapter, a report) since initial and final impressions can have a psychological impact on the reader. (If you look back at the last exercise, you'll see that the threat to the reader's employment – though expressed as a dependent clause – is the last thought expressed in the message. As such, it has been given psychological emphasis.)

- State the importance of your subject and/or devote more space to it within a given sentence space, paragraph, or chapter than to other ideas.

- Link visual or emotional trigger terms to it.

You <u>deemphasize</u> your subject psychologically when you do the following:

- Bury it in the middle of a particular body of text (i.e., a sentence, a paragraph, a section, a chapter).

- Verbally downplay its importance and/or devote less space to it in a section of text than to other ideas.

- Do not link visual or emotional trigger terms to it.

Psychological emphasis requires reading rather than simple scanning, and you must analyze the writing more closely to see how the main ideas have been presented. However, it is an objective treatment that can be analyzed and corrected fairly easily.

<u>To revise your writing for psychological emphasis, follow this 5-step process</u>:

Step 1: Read the message and **list** the ideas that have been emphasized psychologically, especially by virtue of the visual or emotional triggers that link them to the subject or the reader.

Step 2: Analyze the message closely to identify the subject and purpose of the message **and list** the key points that should have been emphasized or de-emphasized in the message.

Step 3: Compare the two lists to determine what makes sense given the purpose of your message.

Step 4: Plan the revision using the psychological emphasis/ de-emphasis techniques listed above.

Step 5: Revise the text.

<u>Exercise</u>:

Here's part of a letter that a student who owned an orchard received and submitted for comment and review in one of my business writing classes. Scanning won't tell you much since the text is not complete, so go ahead and read it word for word.

Dear Fruit Grower,

RE: XYZ Wind Machines

May we help you improve your profit picture by protecting your fruit growing business from frost damage? I'm sure that it is no fun to grow fruit when there is a short crop. Disaster loans may allow your business to survive, but a full crop in a short crop year returns big profits.

...Investing in wind machines has little risk. In many cases, in high density apple orchards, there can be a one year pay-back. In peaches, there can be a two year pay-back. If, down the road, your orchard becomes a "country estate" or equivalent, used XYZ machines are in big demand...

Step 1: Your list of visual or emotional ideas linked to the subject (wind machines) or to the reader should include the following:

- 👁 frost damage – linked to "your business"

- 👁 short crop – not linked to reader

- 👁 disaster loans – linked to "your business"

- 👁 full crop in a short crop year...big profits – not linked to reader

- 👁 orchard becomes a "country estate" or equivalent – linked directly to reader

Notice that most of these ideas, which would be easy for an orchard owner to imagine, envision, or react to emotionally, are negative.

Step 2: The subject of the message is wind machines, and the purpose of the message is to sell the reader a wind machine. Your list of key points that should have been emphasized should include the following:

- The machine can improve the reader's profit picture by allowing growth of a full crop in a short crop year.
- The machine will pay for itself within a very short time.
- A used machine should sell fairly easily.

Step 3: In comparing the two lists, you may have noticed the following:

- The trigger terms identified in the first list are negative, even though the key ideas identified in the second list are positive.
- The writer has unwittingly focused on disaster and deemphasized the value of the product to be sold.

As it turns out, despite the positive offer of help with which the message begins, the student who submitted this letter – an orchard owner – told the class that she was so discouraged by the letter's content that she would never consider purchasing the product, which now evoked too many negative images in her mind to make investing in it a possibility.

Part of the reason the letter had this effect is that many of the negative ideas were linked directly to the reader, while the positive ideas were linked to no one in particular. You'll learn later in this book that the handling of positive and negative ideas requires special care and that dealing effectively with features and benefits can make your message more persuasive.

Step 4: You should now know what you must do:

☑ Eliminate some of the negatives and focus on the positives, being sure to link those positives to the subject and the reader to encourage identification with them.

Step #5: Here are the original message and a possible revision to which physical and grammatical emphasis techniques have also been applied:

Original version

Dear Fruit Grower,

RE: XYZ Wind Machines

May we help you improve your profit picture by protecting your fruit growing business from frost damage? I'm sure that it is no fun to grow fruit when there is a short crop. Disaster loans may allow your business to survive, but a full crop in a short crop year returns big profits.

...Investing in wind machines has little risk. In many cases, in high density apple orchards, there can be a one year pay-back. In peaches, there can be a two year pay-back. If, down the road, your orchard becomes a "country estate" or equivalent, used XYZ machines are in big demand...

Revised version

Dear Fruit Grower:

We believe we can help you to improve your profit picture and take some of the uncertainty out of your business.

Our product is the XYZ wind machine, and here's how it can benefit your business:

- *You should be able to increase profits using our wind machine since the protection against frost damage the machine affords will make it more likely that you'll be able to harvest a full crop even in a short crop year.*

- *If yours is a high density apple orchard, you'll risk very little by investing in a wind machine since your pay-back could come as soon as one year. In peaches, you could get a two year pay-back.*

- *Furthermore, since used XYZ machines are in big demand, your investment can pay off even when you sell it...*

Notice the ideas linked directly to the subject and/or the reader:

- ✪ Improving the profit picture
- ✪ Taking some of the uncertainty out of the business
- ✪ Increasing profits
- ✪ Harvesting a full crop even in a short crop year
- ✪ Risking little

✪   Receiving a quick pay-back

✪   Receiving a return even at time of resale

Notice, also, how reorganizing the ideas not only creates a positive first impression but makes it possible for you to spot those areas where more detail could be provided to make the letter more persuasive. For instance, explanations could be provided between the bullets to elaborate on the features of the wind machine. Of course, this is only part of the letter, so some of those details were probably provided in the original message, but they were obviously not presented in a way that helped the reader to overcome the negative impression she got when she read the letter.

Watch what you emphasize when you write. The reader is paying attention and will interpret your message based on the images you create.

By the way, you may have noticed that I eliminated the subject line. Since this is a sales letter, the reader benefit should come before the product is mentioned.

What should be emphasized/deemphasized

In using emphasis, the choices you make should be based on your subject, your purpose, and your audience. However, in business communication, the following types of information should almost always be underline emphasized for effectiveness:

•   Positive information, including main points

•   Requests that do not require persuasion

- The reader, reader needs, reader benefits
- Positive links between the reader and the writer
- Justification, in the case of negative information
- Goodwill elements
- A call to action in sales messages

Although these types of information don't necessarily warrant full emphasis in all instances, they should be made more prominent than most other types of information.

Conversely, the following types of information should usually be <u>deemphasized</u>:

- Negative information, unless it is critical to the well-being of the reader or of others
- Insignificant information
- Impersonal material, including "policy" and references to enclosures
- The writer, the writer's needs, writer benefits

As we've seen in the previous examples, emphasizing or deemphasizing the wrong ideas can weaken a message, mislead the reader, and lead to unexpected and unwanted results.

Common mistakes

When you analyze emphasis during the revision process and prepare to use emphasis techniques, you should try to spot and to avoid the following common errors:

- Burying important ideas within paragraphs
- Making negative words or ideas too prominent
- Overusing a particular emphasis technique (e.g., listing, underlining, capitalization)
- Using too many different emphasis techniques unnecessarily
- Using emphasis techniques to highlight meaningless or irrelevant words or ideas

Remember that emphasis techniques lose their effectiveness if they are misapplied, as would be the case if:

- Too many words or ideas are written in bold or are underlined.
- Too many ideas are listed when they should simply be discussed in sentence form.
- Too many sentences include unusual punctuation (e.g., parentheses, dashes, or exclamation points).

The effect you create in those situations is similar to the effect you would create by shouting everything you said: Nothing you said would stand out, and the increase in volume and force would only irritate your listeners.

Applying the concept

You are now ready to apply the concept of emphasis in its many forms to the revision process.

Exercise:

The beauty of this first key concept is that it helps you to see how to revise even the simplest letters. The following letter was submitted by a company whose employees participated in a "Key Concepts" seminar series:

Enclosed is your renewal policy for the upcoming term. Please take a moment to review this information to be sure it is correct before placing this with your other important papers. If you should find any item that you do not understand or feel should be corrected, please contact us.

If this renewal should include your auto policy, State identification cards are included to keep in your vehicle.

Thank you for doing business with the XYZ Agency; we appreciate having you as a customer.

P.S. In addition to personal insurance programs, we offer a full line of Life and Health products.

As you can see, this is a fairly well-written letter, but let's see if we can improve it using emphasis techniques.

Step #1: Your list of items that have been emphasized should include the following:

- The items that have been physically emphasized:
  - The "P.S." because of the capitalized initials and the end position
  - The two sentences that have each been given their own paragraph space

- 👁 The independent clauses: (grammatical emphasis)
  - ▸ *Enclosed is your renewal policy for the upcoming term*
  - ▸ *Please take a moment*
  - ▸ *...please contact us*
  - ▸ *...State identification cards are included to keep in your vehicle.*
  - ▸ *Thank you for doing business...*
  - ▸ *...we appreciate having you as a customer.*
  - ▸ *...we offer a full line of Life and Health products*
- 👁 First and last ideas presented (psychological emphasis):
  - ▸ "Enclosed"
  - ▸ "P.S."
- 👁 Emotional or trigger images linked to the product (psychological emphasis):
  - ▸ None.

Step #2: The subject of this letter is the enclosed policy, and the purpose is to convey the message that the reader should inspect the enclosed document and follow certain directions relating to that document.

Your list of what should have been emphasized should include the following:

- 👌 A request that the reader inspect the enclosed document

- Any actions the reader should take regarding the document
- Any reader benefits
- A thank you

Step #3: In comparing your two lists, you'll note the following:

> ➤ The items that have been physically and psychologically emphasized fail to relate clearly to the purpose of the message.

> ➤ Grammatically, the first independent clause, which focuses on the policy, could possibly stop the reader from reading the rest of the letter by implying that the purpose and message are the same: simply to convey a document.

> ➤ The primary actions the reader should perform have been lumped together in the first paragraph and essentially buried because of that fact.

Step #4: We now know the following:

> ☑ This letter could easily be improved simply by shifting the emphasis to help the reader prioritize the ideas and understand them more clearly.

Step #5: See how the original message and the proposed revision compare:

Original version

Enclosed is your renewal policy for the upcoming term. Please take a moment to review this information to be sure it is correct before placing this with your other important papers. If you should find any item that you do not understand or feel should be corrected, please contact us.

If this renewal should include your auto policy, State identification cards are included to keep in your vehicle.

Thank you for doing business with the XYZ Agency; we appreciate having you as a customer.

P.S. In addition to personal insurance programs, we offer a full line of Life and Health products.

Revised Version

Please take a moment to review the enclosed renewal policy to be sure it is correct before placing it with your other important papers.

- *If you should find any item that you do not understand or feel should be corrected, please contact us.*
- *If this renewal includes your auto policy, please be sure to keep the enclosed State identification cards in your vehicle.*

Thank you for doing business with the XYZ Agency. We appreciate having you as a customer.

P.S. In addition to personal insurance programs, we offer a full line of Life and Health products. Please call if we can be of service to you in these important areas of protection.

Notice the use of emphasis in this revision:

- ✪ The first sentence, which begins with a word that directly addresses the reader, focuses on the primary action the reader must take.

- ✪ The secondary actions are emphasized by being linked directly to the reader and by being listed, which should help the reader to check them off as they are completed.

- ✪ The "Thank You" is set off by itself, as it was in the original letter.

- ✪ The P.S. includes a call to action that involves the reader.

As you can see, an understanding of emphasis can help you to revise your writing to improve and strengthen your message with very little effort. The other Key Concepts deal with the types of information that should be emphasized or deemphasized. They, too, are objective and can provide you with the tools necessary to take a lot of the guess work out of the revision task.

Challenge

To discover how easy it is to revise with emphasis in mind, simply pick up any letter on your desk or open any email on your computer and scan it quickly to see what has been emphasized and deemphasized in it. See if you could make immediate recommendations for revising the letter or email that would shift the emphasis to strengthen the message and to lessen the impact of any ideas that might interfere with the writer's purpose.

Please note that revision requires that you have a draft in front of you. Don't try to revise your own work until you have written a draft and turned away from it for at least a few minutes to restore your vision and objectivity. Then begin your revision by looking at emphasis. Try to spot the obvious errors, make note of the changes you must make, and move on to the next concept.

<u>HINT</u>: Don't labor too long or you'll drive yourself crazy and probably destroy your message. Remember that the object of revision is to improve the message, not to make it perfect.

SUZANNE R. ROY

KEY CONCEPT #2: PERSONALIZATION

INTRODUCTION

In order to communicate effectively, you must know not only how to emphasize your message properly but also how to help the reader relate to that message in a positive, productive, and non-threatening way. In other words, you must know when to make the message personal and when to make it impersonal. As a writer, you can make your message more effective by knowing when and how to personalize your writing.

Personalization is a Key Concept because of several factors:

- In today's automated and computerized world, most readers value communication that recognizes them personally, treats them as valued human beings, and gives them a sense that they are dealing with human beings on the other end.

- ☛ Most readers will respond to writing that involves them in the message.

- ☛ Reader response can be controlled to a large extent by the writer's selection of techniques that make the message personal or impersonal.

Like emphasis, personalization can be spotted fairly easily during the revision phase of writing. Once you know what to look for, you'll be surprised to discover how often most writers personalize the wrong type of information and fail to make personal those elements of their message that could elicit favorable responses from the reader. You'll improve the effectiveness of your writing, especially your sales or persuasive correspondence, once you understand this key concept.

MAKING IT PERSONAL/IMPERSONAL

Making your correspondence <u>personal</u> means:

- Recognizing the reader as a person
- Relating the message clearly to the reader
- Involving the reader directly in the message

Conversely, making your correspondence <u>impersonal</u> means:

- Treating the reader as a nameless part of the general public
- Keeping the message separate from the reader
- Not involving the reader directly in the message

You can accomplish either goal through a careful selection of *content, language,* and *form.*

Content:

<u>You make your message personal when you</u>:

- Begin with a cordial greeting *(scannable).*

You wouldn't think of stopping a friend or acquaintance on the street and beginning a conversation without exchanging a friendly greeting with that person. Remember the value of such a greeting when its use is appropriate in written correspondence – even in emails that are not part of a current continuing thread of correspondence.

- Refer to the reader by name *(scannable).*

Most people like to hear their name spoken or see it written, and they respond to the sound or sight of their name immediately. Just be sure you have it right.

- Focus on the reader's needs, situation, desires.

People find their own needs of prime interest, so you'll get them involved in your message if you make it clear that you understand those needs and recognize their importance.

- Refer to specifics that apply to the reader's background.

People like to be recognized for who they are and will often respond positively to those who've taken the time to discover their background.

- Help the reader to visualize personally reacting to, using, or benefiting from the product or subject being discussed.

A reader who can connect with your message will probably react to it more strongly than one who can't.

- Involve the reader in the action.

People are likely to take action if they are directed to do so and if they are allowed to see themselves doing so.

- End cordially *(scannable)*.

Just as you wouldn't begin a conversation without a greeting, you wouldn't just walk away at the end without some sort of cordial goodbye. Remember to end your correspondence cordially when it is appropriate to do so. Even emails, unless they are part of a current continuing thread, should contain some kind of friendly sign-off.

You make a message less personal or even impersonal when you:

- Get to business immediately *(scannable)*.

By presenting the information without establishing some sort of rapport with the reader, you give the reader the message that this encounter is strictly business.

- Do not refer to the reader by name *(scannable)*.

By keeping name references out of the correspondence, you send a signal that the reader's identity is of little consequence to you or to your message.

- Make no reference to the reader's background.

By ignoring the reader's background, you send the message that it is irrelevant in this situation.

- Do not establish a link between the reader and the product or subject being discussed.

By establishing distance between the reader and the product, you send a message that the product should be viewed objectively and impersonally.

- Focus exclusively on business, relying heavily on data.

By focusing on the facts and on statistics, you let the reader know that human considerations such as feelings and desires have little relevance to your message.

- Do not focus on the reader's needs, situation, desires.

By avoiding mention of the reader's needs and desires, you make clear that the reader's personal involvement in your message is not important.

- Leave the reader out of the action.

However, be aware that, by not involving the reader in the action, you risk not getting a response from the reader.

- End on a business note *(scannable)*.

By ending in this way, you reinforce the impersonal nature of the encounter.

Language

<u>Elements of language that you can use to personalize your message include</u>:

- Personal pronouns and adjectives - *I, me, my, mine, you, your, yours, we, us, our, ours,* etc. *(scannable)*

These words help to humanize the message and to establish links between the reader and the writer.

- Everyday language, including contractions - *I'll,* for example, instead of *I will (scannable)*

Be sure that you know your reader's desires and expectations and that you remain consistent with the overall purpose and tone of your message. Avoid slang or jargon unless their appropriateness is very clear.

- Use of voice *(scannable for the presence or absence of the verb "to be" as an auxiliary)*

Voice can be used to control the focus of the message and how the reader will identify with negative information.

<u>Elements of language that you can control to make the message impersonal or less personal include</u>:

- Passive voice *(scannable)*

Selective use of the passive voice can allow you to leave yourself and the reader out of the message and to focus exclusively on the message itself.

- Formal language or language that is intrinsically impersonal *(scannable)*

Use of language that is canned or stiff will make it clear that your focus is on the message and not on the individual reader. Words such as "record" and "policy" and phrases such as "per your request" and "enclosed please find" create a very impersonal tone, especially when they are used in positions of emphasis.

Form:

You make your message more personal when you:

- Present your message in an original, "non-formatted" way *(scannable)*

Most people receive form letters every day and recognize how truly impersonal they are. Personalized presentations are usually seen as being more friendly and sincere.

You make your message less personal when you use:

- Form letters or other pre-formatted materials

Use of such formats will make it clear that your focus is on getting the message out and not on personalizing it for the reader.

To revise your writing for personalization, I recommend the following 5-step revision process:

Step 1: Scan the message **and list** the key ideas that have been personalized.

Step 2: Analyze the message more closely to determine its subject and its purpose **and list** all the key points that should be personalized in the message.

Step 3: Compare the two lists to determine what has been personalized, what should have been personalized and, if applicable, what should have been made less personal in the message.

Step 4: Plan the revision based what you've discovered in comparing the two lists.

Step 5: Revise the text.

Exercise:

Here is part of a letter submitted by a student as sample material:

> *A district and region poster contest is being held to encourage you and your family to think about what safety means to you. The guidelines for this contest will be handed out during a PCM announcing safety week. There will be a contest winner in each district. The winning district posters will be forwarded to the region.*

Step #1: Your list of ideas that have been personalized should include the following:

- 👁 Encouragement to think about safety – as evidenced in the use of the personal pronouns and adjectives "you," "your," and "you" in connection with that idea

Since this is only part of a letter, there is no greeting or cordial ending and the reader has not been referred to by name.

Perhaps you also noted the following phrases that made use of the passive voice:

- ▸ "*is being held*," "*will be handed out*," and "*will be forwarded*"

In your analysis, be sure to take note of the effect of these phrases on the overall tone of the message.

Step #2: The subject of the text is the announcement of the company-sponsored poster contest, and the purpose seems to be to inform and perhaps to persuade the reader to take part in the contest. Your list of what should have been personalized should include:

- Why the contest might interest the reader
- How the reader can take part in the contest

Step #3: In comparing the two lists, you probably noted the following:

- ➢ The process of entering the contest has not been linked to the reader in a personal way.
- ➢ There does seem to be an attempt in the first sentence to involve the reader in the message. However, the use of personal pronouns to refer to the reader ends after the first sentence. Why does the reader suddenly disappear? And what about the reader's interests, needs, etc.? They have disappeared, too.

> ➤ The personal element of the message has been further weakened by the use of the passive voice in this paragraph. Although the passive voice can be used selectively to keep the focus on the reader, this should be done only if the active voice will not allow such a focus or if there are other reasons for using the passive voice. Here, the use of the passive voice has totally hidden the writer from view and almost eliminated the reader from the paragraph as well.

> ➤ Finally, you may have noticed that the writing is very formal and that the writer has not made use of contractions at all. Given the nature of the message, this formality makes the message seem stiff.

Step #4: To personalize this paragraph, we now know the following:

> ☑ We'll have to make the writing less passive and add more personal pronouns to involve the reader in the message.

> ☑ We might also consider making the writing a bit less formal.

Step #5: Here's how a possible revision of the message would compare with the original:

Original version

A district and region poster contest is being held to encourage you and your family to think about what safety means to you. The guidelines for this contest will be handed out during a PCM announcing safety week. There will be a contest winner in each district. The winning district posters will be forwarded to the region.

Revised version

To encourage you and your family to think about what safety means to you, we plan to hold a district and regional poster contest and hope you'll get your entire family involved!

You'll receive the guidelines for this contest during a PCM announcing safety week. The contest should not only be a fun way to teach your family about safety, but think how proud you'd be to see your family's winning poster displayed in your district and at the regional office as well.

Since we'll be choosing a contest winner in each district, your odds of being selected should be pretty good. We hope you'll join us in making this contest a success.

Good luck!

The difference in personalization between the two messages should be clear, even during a quick scan of the text, since the more abundant use of personal pronouns and the direct involvement of the reader can be seen at a glance.

Here's another exercise:

Dear Father,

In checking our records, we have found you have not yet returned the Parish Council form. I have enclosed a copy for your convenience. If you have already returned this form, I thank you.

Would you please fill this out and return it immediately to my attention.

Thank you for your cooperation in this matter.

Step #1: Your list of the ideas that have been personalized should include the following:

- The salutation
- Failure to return a form
- The convenience of the enclosure
- The "Thank you"
- The request for action

Step #2: The subject of this letter is the Parish Council form being conveyed, and the purpose is to get the reader to return the enclosed form as soon as possible.

Your list of the points that should be personalized should include:

- The need to return the enclosed form
- The urgency of the request

Your list of what should not be personalized should include:

- The fact that the reader has not returned the form

Step #3: In comparing your lists, here's what you may have noted:

> The negative has been personalized, possibly to the detriment of reader reaction and/or response.

Step #4: Now we know the following:

☑ This letter should be a straightforward request since there's an urgency to it.

☑ Any reference to the reader's possible error should be kept as impersonal as possible.

Step #5: Here's a possible revision:

Dear Father:

Please fill out the enclosed Parish Council form and return it <u>immediately</u> to my attention.

Our records indicate that we never received this form from your parish. However, if you've already submitted it, please call me or resubmit the information.

Thank you for your cooperation in this matter.

Notice the following changes:

✪ The emphasis has been corrected: The request has been placed at the beginning, and the word "*immediately*" has been stressed.

✪ Also, the reader has been allowed to save face by being told that the form was not received, which could mean that the problem was not necessarily the reader's fault.

✪ The use of "*records*" helps to maintain the impersonal nature of the discovery.

What Should Be Personalized/Impersonalized

As with emphasis, the choices you make in applying personalization to your writing should be affected by your subject, your purpose, and your audience. However, in business communication, the following types of information should almost always be personalized for effectiveness:

- Goodwill messages
- Persuasive requests
- Sales information
- Buffers, justification, and endings in negative messages
- Warnings or imminent danger that the reader must pay attention to

Conversely, the following types of information should almost always be impersonalized:

- Strictly routine messages

- General directions
- Strictly negative information that does not present an imminent danger to the reader
- Most formal report text (depending on purpose and audience)

Common mistakes

When you analyze personalization during the revision process and prepare to use personalization techniques, you should try to spot and to avoid the following common errors:

- Overuse of the reader's name, which can sound insincere or even be annoying
- Improper use of informal language (Hint: Know your reader, and write in an appropriate tone)
- Use of inappropriate personal information that might make the reader feel that his/her privacy has been violated
- Misinterpretation of the reader's needs, desires, etc.
- Unnecessary personal reference to the writer in formal reports

Remember that a personalized message that is inappropriate or threatening to the reader is more damaging than an impersonal form letter. So is a form letter that has been personalized in a way that is obviously mechanical and not personal at all.

Applying the concept

You should now be able to apply the concept of personalization to the revision process.

The following is part of a letter submitted for review:

Here is your long-awaited Specialty Card Care and Maintenance Manual. It is a basic manual explaining how to put away card orders. I tried to be as thorough as possible concerning plan-o-grams, pull tickets, and general information concerning each line. Please have your card person read this manual. If your card person is on vacation or out sick and another associate needs to put product away, be sure he or she reads the appropriate section before doing so. If, after reading the instructions, he or she has any questions, please make sure I am contacted to answer these questions.

Step #1: Your list of ideas that have been personalized should include:

👁 Arrival of the manual and several directives relating to the use of the manual by the reader's card person or card person substitute – as evidenced by the use of the personal adjective "your" and the personal pronoun "you" as the subject understood in the active voice imperatives "please have," "be sure," and "make sure"

Step #2: The subject of this letter is the enclosed manual, and the purpose seems to be to convey the message that the manual is important and that directions relating to its use must be followed.

♀ Your list of ideas that should be personalized should be blank since this is a technical message that needs no personalization.

Step #3: Although this letter deals with impersonal material, your first list indicates clearly that the letter was personalized.

> ➤ Such personalization actually distracts from a purely technical message. (Personalization, by the way, is a common error in formal reports.)

The passive voice, for instance, could have been used to advantage to remove the focus from the writer and keep the spotlight on the message. Keeping things impersonal is especially important in the giving of directions, where a personal approach could irritate the reader by sounding too dictatorial.

Step #4: To revise this letter, we should:

> ☑ Make it as impersonal as possible by focusing on the message and not on the reader or the writer.

Step #5: Here is a preliminary revision to render this message impersonal:

The enclosed, long-awaited Specialty Card Care and Maintenance Manual is a basic manual explaining how to put away card orders. Every attempt has been made to be sure that plan-o-grams, pull tickets, and general line information are accurate and complete. All card persons should read this manual, and their vacation or sick-leave replacements who are responsible for putting product away should read the appropriate section of this manual. Any questions regarding this manual should be directed to _____.

Notice the following:

✪ The absence of personal pronouns and adjectives, which make it immediately evident that this is not meant to be a personal message

✪ Also, the use of the passive voice ("every attempt has been made..." and "questions...should be directed"), which helps to shift the focus to the message itself

Once Key Concept #2 has been applied to this letter, we can then see how the message could be improved with the use of the emphasis techniques we learned in Chapter 1.

Here's how a final revision would compare with the original:

<u>Original version</u>

Here is your long-awaited Specialty Card Care and Maintenance Manual. It is a basic manual explaining how to put away card orders. I tried to be as thorough as possible concerning plan-o-grams, pull tickets, and general information concerning each line. Please have your card person read this manual. If your card person is on vacation or out sick and another associate needs to put product away, be sure he or she reads the appropriate section before doing so. If, after reading the instructions, he or she has <u>any</u> questions, please make sure I am contacted to answer these questions.

Revised version

The enclosed, long-awaited Specialty Card Care and Maintenance Manual is a basic manual explaining how to put away card orders.

- *All card persons should read this manual.*

- *Their vacation or sick-leave replacements who are responsible for putting product away should read the appropriate section of this manual.*

Every attempt has been made to be sure that plan-o-grams, pull tickets, and general line information are accurate and complete. Any questions regarding this manual should be directed to _____ .

Challenge

Knowing when to make things personal and when to keep them impersonal is key to effective communication. Look back at the correspondence you've sent or received recently and see if you can spot ways in which you could have improved those messages by applying what you now know about this important Key Concept.

KEY CONCEPT #3: FEATURES & BENEFITS

The concepts discussed thus far deal with revision techniques that can help you to assess quickly and objectively how your message is being conveyed and what you can do to make it more effective. They rely on your understanding of your message and of the reader(s) you are addressing.

The third key concept relates to a specific type of message common in most business communication: the persuasive or sales message. It should be applied to all messages that, in whole or in part, attempt to elicit action from the reader. You've actually -- though perhaps unknowingly -- identified features and benefits in the previous chapters, so you're not likely to find this concept difficult at all to apply.

In order to emphasize and personalize your message properly, you must know what you are trying to say and what will be perceived by your readers as positive and beneficial to them. One key element in arriving at such knowledge is to understand the difference between "features" and "benefits" with regard to your subject, and to use this information appropriately. This is what Key Concept #3 deals with.

Features/Benefits is a Key Concept because of several factors:

- You must be able to identify the features of your subject in order to communicate quickly and clearly.

- You must be able to differentiate between features and reader benefits to get the desired reader reaction.

- Most readers will react most favorably to what will benefit them in your message.

This concept could actually be listed as Key Concept #1 for sales communication since the text analysis it requires should be done at the beginning of the revision period. However, the application of the first two concepts can actually help you with this process if you choose to stick to the order presented in this text.

RECOGNIZING FEATURES

The term "features" refers to the specifics of your subject (i.e., the product, service, or idea you are "selling"), including, as applicable:

- A description of it
- Statistics about it
- Its parts or components
- Its most important aspects
- Its capacity or scope
- Its historical background
- Its age
- The method of operation or use associated with it
- Its cost
- Its by-products
- Its location and availability
- Its level of quality
- The people associated with it, as well as their background, skills, education, and experience

Most readers want to know about the specific features of the subject of the communication in order to be able to make an informed decision about that subject.

RECOGNIZING BENEFITS

The term "benefits," on the other hand, refers to the good that the reader (or someone the reader is interested in other than the writer) will derive from the features of the product, service, or idea.

Benefits deal with how features will:

- Meet the reader's basic human needs for:
  - Nourishment
  - Security
  - Belonging
  - Individuality
  - Self-esteem
  - Public acclaim
  - Success
  - Wisdom
- Help the reader reach specific goals
- Simplify the reader's life, job, or task
- Help the reader realize specific desires or dreams
- Affect the reader positively
- Improve the reader's life, job, or image
- Profit the reader

Since not all readers can translate features into specific benefits, you must assist them to be sure that they identify positively with your sales message.

Common Errors

In applying this concept, try to avoid the following mistakes:

- Including useless or minor information about your subject

- Claiming a benefit without providing features to back up the claim

- Incorrectly assessing what the reader values

To revise your writing for features/benefits, I recommend the following 5-step revision process:

Step 1: Scan the message **and list** the features of the idea, item, or service being focused on in the message.

Step 2: Analyze the message more closely to determine its subject and purpose, **and list** any benefits that you think would specifically link the features to the reader.

Step 3: Compare the two lists to determine the benefits that may have been overlooked in the message.

Step 4: Plan the revision based what you've discovered in comparing the two lists.

Step 5: Revise the text.

Exercise:

Here is a letter from an insurance agency. Please read it carefully.

> *Enclosed is your Automobile renewal policy from the ABC Insurance Company. We have not enclosed a bill.* <u>*All billings will come to you directly from the ABC Insurance Company.*</u> *Please make all payments directly to them using the envelopes provided.*
>
> *You will have the opportunity to choose a payment plan to suit your needs. The options will include: full payment or 30% down with quarterly installments.*

Step #1: Your list of features should include the following:

- 👁 Direct billing from the company
- 👁 Envelopes provided for direct payment to the company
- 👁 Choice of two payment plans

Step #2: The subject of the letter is a new billing system, and the purpose is to elicit a specific action from the reader as a result of the change in the way payments should now be made. Your list of potential reader benefits might include the following:

- 🔎 The reader may be served more efficiently as a result of direct billing
- 🔎 Envelopes were included for the reader's convenience

- The expanded payment plan options will provide the reader with more flexibility in paying insurance premiums

Step #3: After reviewing the letter, you should have noted the following:

> None of the potential reader benefits you came up with were attached to the features you found discussed in the letter. In fact, no features were interpreted in terms of reader benefit at all.

Step #4: We now know what needs to be done:

☑ Identifying the reader benefits associated with the features should allow you to strengthen the letter to elicit a positive reaction from the reader:

Step #5: Here are the original message and one possible revision:

<u>Original version</u>

Enclosed is your Automobile renewal policy from the ABC Insurance Company. We have not enclosed a bill. <u>All billings will come to you directly from the ABC Insurance Company.</u> Please make all payments directly to them using the envelopes provided.

You will have the opportunity to choose a payment plan to suit your needs. The options will include: full payment or 30% down with quarterly installments.

Revised version

In order to better serve you and to provide you with expanded payment options, we have streamlined our billing process.

- *Beginning immediately, all billings for the enclosed Automobile policy will come to you directly from the ABC Insurance Company.*

- *This billing system will provide you with the opportunity to choose a payment plan to suit your needs. The payment options will include: full payment, or 30% down with quarterly installments.*

Please make all future payments to the ABC Insurance Company using the envelopes that we've enclosed for your convenience.

Applying the Concept

Here's part of a letter written to promote a counseling center:

Dear

We are writing to introduce XYZ COUNSELING CENTER, which provides psychotherapy and career counseling for individuals, families, couples and groups.

The five professionals at the Center are trained and experienced in a variety of counseling areas and disciplines. Two are Licensed Psychologists, one is a Nationally Certified Career Counselor...

*We have expertise in working with such issues as **co-dependency, adult children of alcoholics...** We also provide consultation to industry, organizations, communities and groups. In addition to private and third party payment, we offer some services on a low fee basis.*

*We have taught at both the undergraduate and graduate levels, and we have extensive experience conducting **workshops and seminars**. We are available to present programs on such topics as:*

Family dynamics and   Personal and spiritual growth...

If you would like further information on our services, please call us at...

Step #1: Your list of features should include the following items:

- 👁 The center provides psychotherapy and career counseling for individuals, families, couples and groups.
- 👁 Five professionals work at the center.
- 👁 These professionals are trained in a variety of counseling areas and disciplines.
- 👁 They have expertise in working with a variety of issues.
- 👁 They provide consultation to industry, organizations, communities and groups.
- 👁 They accept private and third party payment as well as providing some services on a low fee basis.

- They have taught at both the undergraduate and graduate levels and have extensive experience conducting workshops and seminars.

Step #2: This letter's subject is counseling services, and its purpose is to persuade the reader that the XYZ Counseling Center is a valuable resource that can provide the reader with help. Your list of possible reader benefits should include the following:

- The reader could rely on the center's staff because of its experience and education.

- The reader could turn to the center as a real. resource for the family and the community because of the variety of help available there.

- The reader would have payment options tailored to his/her needs.

- The reader could even have group education needs met at the center.

Step #3: A comparison of the two lists should have revealed the following:

- No reader benefits are spelled out or even implied.

Step #4: Now that you see more clearly how readers can benefit from the message, you know how the letter needs to be revised.

- ☑ All features must be presented in terms of reader benefits.

Step #5: Here are the original message and one possible revision:

Original version

Dear

We are writing to introduce XYZ COUNSELING CENTER, which provides psychotherapy and career counseling for individuals, families, couples and groups.

The five professionals at the Center are trained and experienced in a variety of counseling areas and disciplines. Two are Licensed Psychologists, one is a Nationally Certified Career Counselor...

*We have expertise in working with such issues as **co-dependency, adult children of alcoholics...** We also provide consultation to industry, organizations, communities and groups. In addition to private and third party payment, we offer some services on a low fee basis.*

*We have taught at both the undergraduate and graduate levels, and we have extensive experience conducting **workshops and seminars**. We are available to present programs on such topics as:*

Family dynamics and   Personal and spiritual growth...

If you would like further information on our services, please call us at...

Revised version

Dear

*Life, with all its stresses, can sometimes overwhelm even the strongest among us. If you are currently looking for **counseling services** for yourself as an individual or with your significant other, for your family, or for your business, we can provide you with the assistance you need.*

ABC COUNSELING CENTER is a multi-service psychotherapy and career counseling resource ready to serve you and your community. You'll find that we are prepared to help you meet life's challenges without creating additional unnecessary stress in your life.

At ABC Counseling Center:

- *You'll be able to rely on our experienced staff.*

The five professionals who staff the center are trained and experienced in a variety of counseling areas and disciplines. Two are Licensed Psychologists, one is a Nationally Certified Career Counselor....

- *You'll be able to find help in a variety of areas.*

*We have expertise in working with such specialized areas as **co-dependency and adult children of alcoholics,** and we are also prepared to help you with family dynamics, personal and spiritual growth, and career issues.*

- *You'll be able to arrange for payment options that suit you.*

We accept both private and third party payment. In addition, we also offer some services on a low fee basis.

- *You'll even be able to make arrangements for Group Programs.*

*We have taught at both the undergraduate and graduate levels, have extensive experience conducting **workshops and seminars** on a variety of topics, and also provide **consultation** to industry, organizations, communities, and groups.*

Everyone needs outside help when things get tough. For further information about our services, please call...

As you can see, being able to identify benefits can help you to make your letters more personal and more persuasive.

Challenge

Whenever you shop for or purchase a new product or service, make a point of differentiating between its features and the benefits you will gain from those features. This should help you to master this Key Concept and make your writing more effective.

SUZANNE R. ROY

KEY CONCEPT #4: POSITIVE/NEGATIVE

It's important to be able to distinguish between positive and negative messages in order to make optimal use of all of the other Key Concepts discussed in this text. Indeed, knowing whether negative or positive information is affecting the message is critical to communicating effectively. Such knowledge calls for an understanding of the reader's point of view and an awareness of the factors that affect how the reader will perceive the message you are sending.

Positive/Negative is a Key Concept because of the following reasons:

- Readers generally react positively to positive information and negatively to negative information.

- Positive reactions normally lead to positive results, and negative reactions normally lead to negative results, especially in business correspondence.

🔑 The writer can usually influence the reader's reaction through the conscious handling of positive and negative information.

Identifying positives and negatives requires thoughtful analysis of the text. However, as with all of the Key Concepts, the elements can be objectively identified.

MAKING IT POSITIVE/NEGATIVE

Making your correspondence more positive involves making use of *content, language* and *tone* to:

- Emphasize and personalize those elements that the reader is likely to perceive as positive; and

- Either turn into positives those elements that the reader might perceive as negative, or make sure that those elements are de-emphasized and impersonal.

These steps will require the use of the other Key Concepts discussed in the rest of the text.

Content

You move your message toward the <u>positive</u> when you:

- Write about what can be done, what you do have, what will work.

- Help the reader to identify with benefits.

- Simplify actions or steps to be taken.

- Appeal to positive emotions.

- Try to accommodate the reader.
- Deemphasize and impersonalize problems and complications.
- Do not needlessly remind the reader of negative effects.
- Offer hope or, better yet, a concrete alternative or solution to the problem at hand.

Conversely, you move your message toward the <u>negative</u> when you:

- Write about what can't be done, what you don't have, what will not work.
- Fail to help the reader identify with benefits.
- Unnecessarily complicate actions or steps to be taken.
- Appeal to negative emotions.
- Don't make an attempt to accommodate the reader.
- Emphasize and personalize problems and complications.
- Needlessly remind the reader of negative effects.
- Offer no hope, alternative, or solution to the problem at hand.

Language and tone

In using language and establishing tone, you make the message more <u>positive</u> when you:

- Begin and end on a friendly and cordial note. *(scannable)*
- Use positive terms and transitions. *(scannable)*
- Subordinate negative information.
- Inquire rather than accuse.
- Do not threaten, scold, or scare.
- Do not apologize unnecessarily.
- Anticipate positive reactions.
- Give the reader the benefit of the doubt.

Conversely, in using language and establishing tone, you make the message more <u>negative</u> when you:

- Begin and end on an impersonal or unfriendly note *(scannable)*.
- Use negative terms and transitions *(scannable)*.
- Present negative information in your independent clauses.
- Accuse rather than inquire.
- Threaten, scold, or scare the reader.
- Apologize unnecessarily.
- Anticipate negative reactions.
- Fail to give the reader the benefit of the doubt.

<u>To revise your writing for positive/negative effect, I recommend the following 5-step revision process</u>:

Step 1: Scan the message **and list** the positive and/or negative elements in the message.

Step 2: **Analyze** the message more closely to determine its subject and its purpose, **and list** all the key points that should be presented positively and/or negatively in the message.

Step 3: Compare the two lists to determine what should have been presented positively and/or negatively in the message.

Step 4: Plan the revision based on what you've discovered in comparing the two lists.

Step 5: **Revise** the text.

Let's take a look at the following financial institution letter submitted by one of my students as a sample for discussion.

> *This is to notify you that the Association does reserve the right to close out checking accounts that are delinquently overdrawn.*
>
> *Your checking account # _____ has been overdrawn since _____ in the amount of _____.*
>
> *If you do not maintain a working balance by _____ we will close out your account.*
>
> *Yours truly,*

Step #1: Your list of the positives and negatives in the letter should include the following:

◉ Closing the checking account - negative

- 👁 The fact that the account is overdrawn - negative
- 👁 The possibility of not maintaining a working balance - negative
- 👁 The closing of the account - negative
- 👁 The complimentary close - positive

Step #2: The subject of the letter is the status of the customer's account, and the purpose is to convey the message that the customer must take action to avoid having the account closed. Your list of items that should be presented positively and personalized should include the following:

- ? The required actions that the customer must take

Your list of items that should be presented negatively and impersonally include:

- ? The problem – i.e., the overdrawn account
- ? The negative action that might be taken against the customer by the bank

Step #3: Based on the comparison of the two lists, you now know the following:

> The fact that the account is overdrawn, which must be expressed clearly even though it is a negative so that the customer does not ignore it, has been expressed in the impersonal passive voice, which did help to avoid putting the customer on the defensive.

➢ The action request was spelled out and personalized, but it was couched in negative language.

➢ The closing of the account, a negative, was personalized, which probably elicited a negative reaction from the customer toward the bank.

You may also have noted the following:

➢ The absence of a personal salutation (calling the reader by name) makes this letter seem unfriendly and impersonal from the very beginning.

➢ The form-letter quality of the letter makes the entire message seem impersonal.

➢ The personalization of the assertion of the bank's rights in the very first sentence makes the letter seem unfriendly.

➢ The absence of an offer to answer questions also makes the letter seem unfriendly.

➢ The "Yours Truly" after such a negative message could elicit a negative reaction from the reader.

These elements conflict with the repeated use of the personal pronouns to produce a message that is at once threatening and irritating.

As mentioned earlier, the only technique that's been used correctly is the use of the passive voice with the negative term "*overdrawn*". The writer has refrained from involving the reader directly in the negative action of overdrawing the account. This technique should have been used, if possible, to deal with every negative idea in this letter.

Step #4: Based on this analysis, you can conclude the following:

- ☑ A personal salutation should be used since this will help establish a friendly tone and make the letter seem non-threatening.

- ☑ This letter should be a clear warning and "call to action" message that involves the reader.

- ☑ Any negative actions by either the reader or the writer should remain impersonal to avoid "blame" reactions.

- ☑ An offer of assistance should be included and personalized.

- ☑ The complimentary close should not be overly personal because of the basic message.

Step #5: Here are the original letter and one possible revision: (A friendly, more personal opening paragraph could be added for those special customers that you truly value.)

<u>Original version</u>

This is to notify you that the Association does reserve the right to close out checking accounts that are delinquently overdrawn.

Your checking account # _____ has been overdrawn since _____ in the amount of _____.

If you do not maintain a working balance by
_____ we will close out your account.

Yours truly,

Revised version

Dear Mr. Jones:

The Association's records reveal that your account has been overdrawn since _____ in the amount of _____.

- *To avoid a close-out of checking account #_____, you must restore and maintain a working balance in that account by _____.*

If you have any questions, please call 555-5555. We'll do our best to assist you in dealing with this situation.

Sincerely,

Notice the following:

✪ The salutation sets a personal but formal tone.

✪ The first sentence focuses on impersonal records that perform the nonthreatening action of revealing the problem.

✪ The action of overdrawing is again expressed in the passive voice to avoid blaming the reader.

✪ The call to action is personal and deals with what can be done, not what should not be done.

✪ The offer of assistance comes directly from the writer and is linked directly to the reader; it is personalized through the use of personal pronouns and provides a positive follow-up to the negative information.

✪ The complimentary close is friendly but formal and does not sound false.

As you can see, even a short letter can need substantial revision to make it more effective.

Here's another exercise:

Dear _____:

Thanks for your letter of June 7th.

I don't know where you got the idea that your new store was the prime candidate for the next lottery machine. I was just made aware of the application last week.

We currently have a moratorium on installing new terminals, until we get some new site selection software operating which we believe will assist us in determining the best locations for installing additional terminals to increase revenues for the state.

On the face of it your proposed new location seems to warrant consideration. We'll give it a careful review when the moratorium is lifted in the near future.

Sincerely,

Step #1: Your list of positives and negatives in this letter will probably include the following:

- A cordial greeting and ending - positive

- A thank you - positive

- The fact that the writer doesn't know where the reader got the idea… – negative, personalized ("I", "you"), and possibly insulting

- The moratorium – negative and personalized ("we")

- New software that should help – positive

- The fact that the reader's proposal warrants consideration and will be reviewed – positive

Step #2: The subject of the message is lottery terminals, and the purpose is to inform the reader that the submitted application will be reviewed as soon as the new system is set up. Your list of items that should be presented positively and personalized should include the following:

- What can be done in answer to the reader's request – positive

- Justification for any delay - positive

You may have also noticed the following:

- The accusatory and scolding first paragraph after the thank you is almost a slap in the face to the reader.

- Words or phrases like "I don't know" and "moratorium" signal potential problems.

- ▸ Notice that these elements have been emphasized by being placed at the beginning of their respective paragraphs.
- ▸ They've also been personalized by being linked directly to the writer.

🔍 The emphasis is on what can't be done: "we have a moratorium" translates to "we can't install new terminals."

🔍 To make matters worse, the positive information (the merits of the application and the writer's willingness to review it) has been subordinated to the point where its positive quality is not recognizable.

As you recall from Chapter 1, ideas are subordinated when they are presented in dependent (subordinate) clauses. In this example, the following sentence has one main (independent) clause and two dependent (subordinate) clauses:

- ▸ "*We currently have a moratorium on installing new terminals*" (independent) "*until we get some new site selection software operating*" (dependent) "*which we believe will assist us in determining the best locations for installing additional terminals to increase revenues for the state*" (dependent).

It is consistent with the overall tone of this letter that the main clause focuses on what can't be done and the dependent clauses focus on what is being done and on the positive benefits of those actions.

Step #3: In assessing what you've discovered, you will probably have noted the following:

> ➢ The overall message has the potential to be positive but has been presented in a negative tone.

Step #4: Clearly, to revise this letter, we must:

☑ Focus on and personalize the positive elements of the message.

☑ Subordinate and render impersonal any unavoidable negative information.

Step #5: Here's the original version followed by a possible revision:

<u>Original version</u>

Dear _____ :

Thanks for your letter of June 7th.

I don't know where you got the idea that your new store was the prime candidate for the next lottery machine. I was just made aware of the application last week.

We currently have a moratorium on installing new terminals, until we get some new site selection software operating which we believe will assist us in determining the best locations for installing additional terminals to increase revenues for the state.

On the face of it your proposed new location seems to warrant consideration. We'll give it a careful review when the moratorium is lifted in the near future.

Sincerely,

Revised version

Dear _____:

Thanks for your letter of June 7th.

Your application as a proposed location for a lottery machine reached my desk last week and seems to warrant consideration. I'll review it carefully as soon as the commission resumes its site selection function.

We are currently in the process of placing new site selection software in operation. We believe this software will assist us in determining the best locations for installing additional lottery terminals to increase revenues for the state.

Rest assured that your application will be reviewed as soon as the new system is in place.

Sincerely,

Please notice the following:

- ✪ The most positive information has been placed at the beginning.
- ✪ The focus is on what can be done or is being done.
- ✪ The basic message that the application will be reviewed has been repeated for emphasis.
- ✪ The letter ends on a positive note.

As a result, we've changed the tone of the letter and lessened the impact of the negative parts of the message.

Exercise:

Notice how the most important part of the following message from an insurance agency has been buried and could be overlooked by the casual reader:

> *Dear*
>
> *This is in reference to the telephone message I left on your answering machine, and to prior cancellation notices you have received.*
>
> *Unless a check dated on or before 1/18/14, in an amount of $264.37, was mailed to XYZ Company, you do not have auto insurance in force with this Agency. In the event you have an accident, or someone driving your car has an accident there will be no coverage with the XYZ Insurance Company.*
>
> *It is most urgent that you contact us immediately about your lack of coverage with XYZ. We did receive a check for $238.93, but this was not the amount asked for.*
>
> *Sincerely,*

Step #1: Your list of positive or negative elements should include the following:

- 👁 The possibility that the reader's insurance has been cancelled – negative

- 👁 The resulting lack of coverage in the event of an accident - negative

- 👁 The fact that the writer did receive a check - positive

👁 The fact that the check that was received was not for the correct amount – negative

Step #2: The subject of the letter is the cancellation of an auto insurance policy, and the purpose is to warn the reader that payment is required immediately to reinstate coverage.

📍 Since this message must focus on the negative in order to accomplish its purpose, the negative information should not only be prominent but should also be personalized. However, to control reader reaction, at least one positive element should be included:

▶ The writer's concern for the reader

Step #3: In comparing your lists, you may have noticed the following:

➢ The basic message of the letter - the warning - is buried in the middle of the text.

➢ The positive part, on the other hand, -- that is, the part dealing with the writer's concern for the reader -- is not included at all.

In fact, this letter is very impersonal and, as such, not likely to have a significant effect on the reader.

Step #4: To be sure that the reader gets the whole message and understands its importance, we should:

☑ Personalize it.

☑ Be sure the whole message is included.

☑ Emphasize the message by means of layout techniques.

Step #5: Here are the original message and a suggested revision:

Original version

Dear

This is in reference to the telephone message I left on your answering machine, and to prior cancellation notices you have received.

Unless a check dated on or before 1/18/14, in an amount of $264.37, was mailed to XYZ Company, you do not have auto insurance in force with this Agency. In the event you have an accident, or someone driving your car has an accident there will be no coverage with the XYZ Insurance Company.

It is most urgent that you contact us immediately about your lack of coverage with XYZ. We did receive a check for $238.93, but this was not the amount asked for.

Sincerely,

Revised version

SUBJECT: *Cancellation of your automobile insurance*

Dear

Did you mail a check to XYZ Insurance Company for $264.37 on or before 1/18/14, as requested?

- *If not, your auto insurance is no longer in force.*

This means that, if you have an accident or someone driving your car has an accident, you will <u>not</u> be covered for damage or liability with the XYZ Insurance Company.

> ***PLEASE NOTE:*** *Although we did receive a check for $238.93, it was not the amount asked for and does <u>not</u> cover the cost of your premium.*

<u>Please contact us immediately</u> about your lack of coverage with XYZ. We'd like to make sure that you have the protection you need.

Sincerely,

Notice how quickly we've gotten to the point in this revision. We've also:

- ✪ Personalized the message to be sure the reader identifies with the problem and seeks a speedy solution to it
- ✪ Tried not to blame the reader
- ✪ Used physical as well as psychological emphasis to really get the important negative message across
- ✪ Ended on a positive note by stressing both the link between the reader and the writer, and the writer's concern for the reader's welfare

This revision should be effective and should also help to strengthen the reader/writer relationship.

What is likely to be perceived as positive or negative

- Change, even if it is ultimately for the better, is often perceived as a negative.

- Cost, even if it is minimal, may be perceived as a negative.

- Requests made of the reader, even if they are easy to carry out, may be perceived as a negative.

- Anything that the reader can benefit from – materially, emotionally, or otherwise – is likely to be perceived as a positive.

- If the reader cannot benefit directly, then anything that can benefit people other than the writer is also likely to be looked upon favorably by the reader.

- Conversely, anything that can cause the reader to suffer or experience some sense of loss – materially, emotionally, or otherwise – is likely to be perceived as negative.

- Also, anything that can cause people other than the writer to suffer or experience some sense of loss will usually also be looked upon unfavorably by the reader.

As you can see, knowing your reader is especially critical to the proper application of Key Concept #4.

Common mistakes

In dealing with positives and negatives, you should try to spot and avoid these common errors:

- Ambiguity – Sometimes a negative message is best rendered in negative terms and will get lost if it is deemphasized.

- Mixed messages – A message in which both positive and negative elements are given equal weight may confuse the reader.

- False positives – Don't force positives where they don't exist.

Applying the concept

Let's take a look a memo submitted for revision.

To: All Personnel

Subject: Immediate Action Required Upon Receipt of Orange Folders

Colored folders circulate throughout the departments on a regular basis, and they have different colors for different reasons. It has been mentioned, quite often, the significance of ORANGE FOLDERS! Although, I have noticed no one really remembers what the orange folder represents. So, I will now reiterate what the purpose of the color orange represents in this plant.

When the Marketing department places an order, there may be something special about the order or that may require special attention. But we don't want to alarm the customer that there may be problems with his order, so marketing assures the customer delivery, on the date, that he has requested. This type of action prompts an ORANGE folder.

To fulfill our customer's needs an orange folder is sent out, for circulation. <u>An orange folder requires immediate and undivided attention</u>! Orange means RUSH! There should be <u>no</u> reason an orange folder should sit on an employee's desk for more than one working day. Orange folders represent first priority. The faster we respond, the faster we get our product out the door to our customers.

It is not my responsibility to "baby sit" the orange folder. Please, when you see ORANGE, respond. Satisfied customers mean business and business means profit.

Thank You.

Step #1: Your list of the positives and negatives in the letter should include the following:

- 👁 The writer's aggravation that no one seems to remember what the orange folders represent - negative

- 👁 The fact that orange folders are used to help fulfill the customers' needs - positive

- 👁 The implication that orange folders sit on employee desks for more than one day - negative
- 👁 The declaration that "babysitting" is not one of the writer's responsibilities - negative
- 👁 The idea that satisfied customers mean business and profit - positive

Step #2: The subject of the memo is the Orange Folders, and the purpose seems to be to convey the message that orange folders require immediate attention. Since this memo has a positive purpose and a neutral message, there is no reason to use a negative approach.

Your list of ideas that could be presented positively should include:

- 𝔮 What can be done to make good use of the folders
- 𝔮 The benefit to the reader of using the orange folders

Step #3: In comparing your two lists, you may have noted the following:

- ➤ Although the writer has gotten to the point quickly in the subject line, the message has been obscured and made to seem complicated by being buried in negative material that is not needed in this memo.

Step #4: We can improve this memo by:

- ☑ Eliminating all the negative ideas that are irrelevant or that are included merely to cast blame

☑ Using emphasis techniques to stress what can or should be done

☑ Personalizing those positive or neutral elements that will allow the writer to involve the reader in the message

Step #5: Let's see how the original message and the revision compare:

Original version

To: All Personnel

Subject: Immediate Action Required Upon Receipt of Orange Folders

Colored folders circulate throughout the departments on a regular basis, and they have different colors for different reasons. It has been mentioned, quite often, the significance of ORANGE FOLDERS! Although, I have noticed no one really remembers what the orange folder represents. So, I will now reiterate what the purpose of the color orange represents in this plant.

When the Marketing department places an order, there may be something special about the order or that may require special attention. But we don't want to alarm the customer that there may be problems with his order, so marketing assures the customer delivery, on the date, that he has requested. This type of action prompts an ORANGE folder.

To fulfill our customer's needs an orange folder is sent out, for circulation. <u>An orange folder requires immediate and undivided attention</u>! Orange means RUSH! There

should be <u>no</u> reason an orange folder should sit on an employee's desk for more than one working day. Orange folders represent first priority. The faster we respond, the faster we get our product out the door to our customers.

It is not my responsibility to "baby sit" the orange folder. Please, when you see ORANGE, respond. Satisfied customers mean business and business means profit.

Thank You.

Revised version

To: All Personnel

Subject: Orange Folders = Same-Day Speedy Response

As you may have noticed, the folders that circulate throughout the departments on a regular basis have been color coded. The Marketing department would like to remind everyone that it uses ORANGE folders to call attention to orders that are special or that require special attention.

When you see an ORANGE FOLDER, please remember:

- *The folder requires your immediate and undivided attention.*
- *It contains a rush order.*
- *It represents a first priority.*
- *It demands an immediate, same-day response.*

<u>*In other words, when you see ORANGE, think "RUSH."*</u>

The faster we respond to customer orders, the faster we get our product out the door and the more customers we satisfy. Since satisfied customers mean more business, we all benefit from increased efficiency.

Remember: When you see ORANGE, please respond!

Thank You.

Please notice:

- ✪ All mention of reader forgetfulness or lack of understanding has been eliminated.

- ✪ The focus has been put on the positive message itself and on the reader's response to that message.

The result is a memo that is brief, concise, to the point, easy to understand and to remember, and reader-oriented.

Here's another example:

Subject: Designated Smoking Area

Effective immediately, smoking will be limited to the Dining Room or outside the facility. Once construction has been completed, smoking will be limited to the Offices and the Staff Conference Room. Even though this memo is a direct result of recent Legislation, it has been our intention for some time to limit smoking to that part of the facility which is undergoing construction and not in the living areas because none of the residents smoke. I would tend to view this as a positive step toward maintaining a healthy atmosphere for our residents and I would hope you would share a similar perspective.

Step #1: Your list of positive/negative elements will probably include the following:

- 👁 The new restriction on where to smoke – negative

- 👁 The continuing restriction once construction is completed – negative

- 👁 The fact that none of the residents smoke – potentially negative to a smoker

- 👁 The tentative nature of the writer's assertion about the decision – potentially negative

- 👁 The writer's uncertainty about reader response – potentially negative

Step #2: The subject of the message is a new smoking policy, and the purpose is to inform the reader that smoking will be limited to certain areas of the building. Your list of items that should be expressed as positives should include the following:

- 📍 Where smoking is allowed

- 📍 Any justification for the new policy

- 📍 How the reader will benefit from the change

- 📍 The writer's own attitude toward the change

Step #3: The message is potentially negative but shouldn't be presented as such if the writer wants to secure a positive response from the reader. You should have noted the following:

- ➢ The subject line has been well handled, since it is neutral.

- ➢ Unfortunately, the writer has made the message negative by focusing on the "limiting" aspect of the information and thereby stressing what the reader will no longer be able to do.

- ➢ The positive reasons or justifications are buried in the text.

- ➢ Any personalization is focused primarily on the writer and the writer's association with negative ideas.

Step #4: To improve the message, we should:

- ☑ Place the positive or neutral ideas and justifications at the beginning of the message.

- ☑ Eliminate any personal connection established between the writer and the negative ideas.

- ☑ Focus on what can be done rather than on what can't be done.

- ☑ Enlist the reader's cooperation at the end.

Step #5: Here are the original message and a possible revision:

<u>Original version</u>

Subject: Designated Smoking Area

Effective immediately, smoking will be limited to the Dining Room or outside the facility. Once construction has been completed, smoking will be limited to the Offices and the Staff Conference Room. Even though this memo is a direct result of recent Legislation, it has been our intention for some time to limit smoking to that part of the facility which is undergoing construction and not in the living areas because none of the residents smoke. I would tend to view this as a positive step toward maintaining a healthy atmosphere for our residents and I would hope you would share a similar perspective.

Revised version

Subject: New Designated Smoking Area

To maintain a healthy atmosphere for our residents, none of whom smoke, and to comply with recent legislation and thus avoid potential fines, we are designating the following spaces as exclusive *smoking areas within our facility:*

- *Until construction is finished, the Dining Room will be the designated smoking area.*
- *Once construction has been completed, the designated smoking area will shift from the Dining Room to the Offices and the Staff Conference Room.*

Use of the Dining Room as the exclusive smoking area is effective immediately and will remain in effect until construction is completed. Smoking will no longer be permitted in other parts of the building.

We trust that you will see the value of maintaining the rest of the facility as a "smoke-free" environment for our residents.

We thank you for your cooperation.

<u>Please notice the following</u>:

- ✪ The emphasis is on what can and will be done.

- ✪ Only positive or neutral ideas are personalized by being linked to the reader and the writer.

Challenge

Look back at any message or correspondence you've sent or received recently, and see if you can spot any negative information in the message. Pay particular attention to the mention of what can't be done as opposed to what can be done, and on how personalization has been used with regard to negative ideas or language. You may be surprised to discover how often negative information is conveyed with no attempt to justify it or to minimize its effect on the reader.

KEY CONCEPT #5: COMMON GROUND

Once you've mastered the first four concepts, you're ready to consider how a writer establishes "common ground" with the reader.

You now know that you can make your messages more persuasive by personalizing them and focusing on reader benefits and that turning negatives into positives or somehow minimizing negative reactions to messages can also help you get positive results from your writing. These techniques can be enhanced if you understand how to identify a common ground that you and the reader can stand upon -- that is, a place that makes it clear that both of you share a particular view or see things from the same perspective.

Common ground is a Key Concept because:

- Most people tend to react positively and sympathetically to people who share their point of view.

- Most people are less likely to dismiss ideas quickly if those ideas resemble their own.

- Most people will refrain from "killing the messenger" when bad news is involved if the messenger shares something in common with them.

Since it is primarily negative information that triggers the need to pay special attention to the writer's relationship with the reader, it is in correspondence containing a negative message that you will want to analyze the use of this concept. However, the concept can be applied in any situation that calls for building a bridge between the writer and the reader in order to get a positive response from the reader.

ESTABLISHING COMMON GROUND

You establish common ground when, as applicable, you:

- Mention something you and the reader share or have in common, as evidenced or implied in the subject being discussed or simply as a result of your common bonds as human beings; for example,

- an interest,
- a desire,
- a goal,
- a belief,
- a concern,
- a principle,
- a possession,
- a hobby,
- a job.

- Identify and/or strengthen the relationship you share with the reader as you deliver the message.

- Remind the reader of (and, if appropriate, express gratitude for) something positive and significant that has occurred between you; for example,

  - a contact or the receipt of something not directly related to the negative information you are about to deliver.

- Express appreciation for the reader's concerns, efforts, support, and understanding as those elements relate to something you both believe in.

- Express encouragement or congratulations, or make a positive, relevant comment about the reader or about something or someone connected or related to the reader.

You fail to establish a solid common ground if you

- Do not establish a link between yourself and the reader.

- Ignore any relationship that may exist between you and the reader as you deliver the message. - By maintaining distance from the reader, you make it clear that any relationship that might exist between the two of you is not relevant to your message.

- Deal with negative or irrelevant information before you establish such a connection.

Common mistakes

In dealing with common ground, you should try to spot and avoid these common errors:

- Ambiguity: If the reader is misled into expecting a positive message, the reaction will be twice as negative as it might have been without the buffer.

- Establishing common ground that links the writer and reader with respect to negative ideas

- The use of obvious and pointless flattery

- Irrelevant comments that provide no transition into the message

- False sincerity: Writers should avoid expressing appreciation for or pleasure in something that is not within their realm of concern.

- The use of condescending or patronizing language

- Preachiness

- Scolding

- False identification: Writers should not identify with the reader's situation if they are not in a position to do so.

- Overstatement of concern or involvement: Writers must be careful in equating their level of concern with the reader's.

- Writer-orientation: Writers should never focus primarily or exclusively on themselves.

- Self-defeating statements: Writers should avoid providing the reader with ammunition that can be used against them.

<u>To revise your writing for common ground, I recommend the following 5-step revision process</u>:

Step 1: <u>Scan</u> the message **and list** the obvious links established between the writer and the reader.

Step 2: **Analyze** the message more closely to determine its subject and its purpose, **and list** the key points that lend themselves to establishing common ground between the writer and the reader.

Step 3: Compare the two lists to determine what common ground could have been established and what ideas should not have been used as the basis for common ground.

Step 4: Plan the revision based what you've discovered in comparing the two lists.

Step 5: Revise the message.

<u>Exercise</u>:

Here is a letter written in response to a classroom assignment.

> *Dear Jason:*
>
> *Thank you for inviting me to serve as an officer of the XYZ Club. Our organization's team sprit and can-do attitude serve as a model for other organizations to imitate.*
>
> *Being an active member, I know that serving as a good officer takes much time and work. After a great amount of consideration, I regret to inform you that right now my time and energy are needed elsewhere.*
>
> *I'm sure you will find the right person for the position. In the meantime, if there's anything else I can do for you, please don't hesitate to call.*

Step #1: Your first list should include the following obvious links established between the writer and the reader through the use of 1st and 2nd person pronouns in relation to the same idea:

- 👁 The writer's appreciation for the invitation
- 👁 Shared pride in the organization's qualities
- 👁 The writer's regret at not being able to accept the invitation

- 👁 The writer's conviction that the reader will be able to find the right person to fill the position
- 👁 The writer's offer of additional help

Step #2: The subject of the letter is the offer made to the writer by the XYZ Club, and its purpose is to inform the reader that the writer will not accept the invitation to serve as an officer of the club. Your list of natural areas of common ground should include the following:

- 𝄞 Membership in the organization
- 𝄞 Shared pride in the organization's qualities
- 𝄞 The desire to do what's best for the organization

Step #3: Since the reader is likely to perceive the message as negative information, you know that it would be wise to establish common ground with the reader <u>before</u> discussing any part of the message. However, the opening paragraph contains a specific mention of the invitation.

In thanking the reader for the invitation in that first paragraph without giving an answer, the writer might unintentionally mislead the reader into expecting a positive response. Such a misconception could make the reader react more negatively to the refusal when it is delivered than if the bad news had been presented right at the beginning.

If you compare the two lists, you'll also discover the following:

- ➢ A connection was made with regard to a negative idea (regret).

- ➤ A connection was made with regard to the writer's offer of help when the writer had just refused to do what the reader asked.

- ➤ Although the second sentence is an obvious attempt to establish common ground by focusing on a shared recognition of the club's strengths, the writer has not used this idea to create a natural transition point from which to deliver his message – i.e., no connection has been made between this idea and the message itself.

- ➤ The last paragraph attempts to restore common ground, but it is self-defeating because it could generate a sarcastic reaction from the reader. After all, the writer has done nothing for the reader to justify offering to do "anything else".

To establish common ground, it's often helpful to go back to your original correspondence and/or conversation with the reader to be able to spot areas of shared concern or interest. In this case, for example, the reader may have tried to persuade you to accept the invitation by stressing how important your dedication to the club truly is. Remember that negative responses usually come after specific requests or attempts at persuasion. The ideas used to justify the request or to persuade you to respond positively can often be used to establish common ground when you must respond negatively, and sometimes even to justify your refusal.

Step #4: To establish common ground, we now know the following:

- ☑ The opening paragraph should focus on shared ideas that can be used as transition points to get to the real message in as positive a way as possible (e.g., by focusing on what can be done).

- ☑ The message should end on a positive or neutral note.

- ☑ Any common ground relating to the negative points in the message should be eliminated.

Step #5: Let's compare the original message with one possible revision:

<u>Original version</u>

Dear Jason:

Thank you for inviting me to serve as an officer of the XYZ Club. Our organization's team sprit and can-do attitude serve as a model for other organizations to imitate.

Being an active member, I know that serving as a good officer takes much time and work. After a great amount of consideration, I regret to inform you that right now my time and energy are needed elsewhere.

I'm sure you will find the right person for the position. In the meantime, if there's anything else I can do for you, please don't hesitate to call.

Revised version

Dear Jason:

The XYZ Club has really made strides during the past year, and I agree with you that the dedication of our membership is our greatest asset.

Like my fellow members, I've always tried to assess accurately my own strengths and weaknesses in order to serve the club well. In the past week, I've done such a reassessment, and I've concluded that, for the moment, given my current personal schedule and professional responsibilities, I can best serve the organization by continuing in my present capacity as a regular club member.

I'm flattered to have been asked to serve as an officer and look forward to the day when I can accept the challenge. In the meantime, my commitment to the club will remain as strong as ever.

I look forward to seeing you at our next meeting. I'm sure our current level of productivity will move us forward into an exciting new season.

Notice, first of all, that the first paragraph doesn't deal with the invitation at all. Instead:

✪ The first sentence focuses on positive ideas that the writer assumes he and the reader share: pride in the club and agreement about the club's greatest asset. These are ideas that should establish a common ground between the two parties.

✪ The second sentence provides the writer with a means of introducing the real message by establishing that, like other members (indirect common ground), the writer is a dedicated member who wants to serve the club in the best possible way. This transition provides the writer with an easy way to justify the refusal.

✪ The refusal, which is presented in terms of what can be done, not what can't be done, is not linked to the reader or used as common ground. Notice that "you" does not appear in the body of the message. The letter has moved from direct common ground to indirect common ground to neutral ground to keep the reader from identifying with what he/she may consider to be negative information.

✪ The last paragraph again avoids mention of the invitation and the refusal and reestablishes common ground by focusing on something positive the writer believes he and the reader share: a belief in the club's forward movement.

Common ground is most effectively established at the very beginning of a message and is reinforced if it is referred to at the end of the same message. However, it is not effective unless it also provides a natural transition into and out of the core message. Therefore, please remember the following:

✪ In editing your writing or the writing of others, focus on the opening and concluding paragraphs to determine whether or not this key concept has been applied, and be sure that the common ground, or buffer zone, that has been established clearly relates to the message being delivered.

✪ You create common ground when, in a separate opening or concluding paragraph that does not involve the core information to be dealt with, you focus on positive or neutral elements that seem most clearly related to the subject being discussed and that will provide you with the best transitional positioning to get into or out of your core message.

✪ In order to create and/or evaluate the "common ground" element, you must clearly identify for yourself the subject of the message being delivered and discover a bond that links both the writer and the reader to that subject.

✪ Often, common ground ideas can be found in the reader's comments to or correspondence with the writer.

✪ The introduction is the most difficult part of the letter to write. Don't attempt it until the body of the letter and the conclusion have been written.

Applying the concept

Here is a letter submitted in one of my writing classes:

Dear

We would like to take this opportunity to congratulate you for having been nominated by your supervisor for ABC University's Student Employee of the Year award. A committee of employers read your nomination, and while you were not selected, we felt it important for you to know your contribution is recognized and valued by those with whom you work.

The field of finalists was representative of the university's very best student employees. I hope your inclusion in this group is a source of pride and reward for you. From our perspective, your nomination is indicative of an impressive level of motivation and achievement. You have contributed much to your employer's operation and, we hope, have gained from the experience.

The Student Employment staff is pleased with the quality of nominees recommended for this award and impressed by the enthusiasm of supervisors in nominating their employees. We take great pleasure in recognizing the unique and valuable contributions you have made.

Once again, please accept our congratulations for this honorable mention and our sincere good wishes for the future.

Step #1: Your first list should include the following obvious links between the writer and the reader:

- 👁 Recognition that the nomination is cause for congratulations

- 👁 The writer's recognition of the reader's contribution

- 👁 The writer's recognition of the reader's level of motivation and achievement

Step #2: The subject of the letter is the Employee of the Year Award and the purpose is to inform the reader that she/he was not selected as Employee of the Year. Your list of natural areas that could be used to establish common ground between the writer and the reader and to create a natural transition point from which to get into the core message should include the following:

- 👂 The impressive level of motivation and achievement of the university student employees

- 👂 The enthusiastic support of supervisors that pleased both the university and the employees

- 👂 The unique and valuable contributions made by the employees

Step #3: In compiling your lists, you may have noticed the following:

- ➤ The entire core message was included in the first paragraph, before any transitional common ground could be established.

> ▶ Could the opening sentence lead the reader to expect the opposite of the core message being conveyed?

Yes, and this makes the negative information that follows that sentence even more painful than it might otherwise have been. Furthermore, most readers will stop reading once the bad news has been delivered or will develop an attitude before getting to any other information, so any attempt on the writer's part to soften the blow or justify the bad news beyond that point will probably be lost.

> ➤ The ideas presented in the second paragraph would have provided an effective transition point into the core message. Instead, they were used after the core message was delivered.

This fact probably struck some disappointed readers as being a bit patronizing since the writer seems to glorify the finalists a moment too late.

> ▶ Could the closing paragraph generate a negative reaction from the reader?

Yes it could. Notice how it deals the reader one more blow by using the deflated term "honorable mention" after the more enthusiastic rhetoric of the middle paragraphs.

> ➤ Finally, the message is very writer-oriented. It focuses too heavily on the writer's pleasure and not clearly enough on the reader's needs.

Step #4: To improve this letter, you now know that you must:

☑ Establish common ground before delivering the bad news.

☑ Make the letter more reader-oriented.

☑ End on positive or neutral ground.

Step #5: Here are the original version and one possible revision:

Original version

Dear

We would like to take this opportunity to congratulate you for having been nominated by your supervisor for ABC University's Student Employee of the Year award. A committee of employers read your nomination, and while you were not selected, we felt it important for you to know your contribution is recognized and valued by those with whom you work.

The field of finalists was representative of the university's very best student employees. I hope your inclusion in this group is a source of pride and reward for you. From our perspective, your nomination is indicative of an impressive level of motivation and achievement. You have contributed much to your employer's operation and, we hope, have gained from the experience.

The Student Employment staff is pleased with the quality of nominees recommended for this award and impressed by the enthusiasm of supervisors in nominating their employees. We take great pleasure in recognizing the unique and valuable contributions you have made.

Once again, please accept our congratulations for this honorable mention and our sincere good wishes for the future.

Revised version

Dear

ABC University's Student Employment staff is grateful for the unique and valuable contributions that you and your fellow nominees for this year's Student Employee of the Year award have made to the University community. We hope that your nomination was a source of pride for you and that your selection as a finalist has been an additional reward for your efforts.

The field of finalists was representative of the university's very best student employees. Because all of you were so impressive, the committee of employers who read the nominations had a difficult time identifying a single winner. Although you were not selected, we'd like you to know that your contribution is recognized and valued by those with whom you work.

From our perspective, your nomination is indicative of an impressive level of motivation and achievement for which you are to be congratulated. You have contributed much to your employer's operation and, we hope, have gained from the experience.

Best wishes for the future.

Please notice the following:

- ✪ The writer has established common ground with the reader in the first paragraph by focusing on the reader's accomplishments and by allowing the reader to recognize the importance of both the general nomination and the selection as a finalist. Although part of the core message (the award) has been mentioned in the first paragraph, there is nothing ambiguous here that might lead the reader to think that she has won the contest.

- ✪ The last sentence of the first paragraph, which focuses on the finalists, provides the writer with a transition point into the message.

- ✪ The negative information is subordinated and is surrounded by positive reinforcement that seems more sincere because it has already been mentioned independent of the contest results.

- ✪ The final paragraph makes no mention of the negative information but again reestablishes common ground by linking the reader and the writer in a positive way.

Challenge

Establishing common ground is probably the most difficult of the Key Concepts to apply. As with most skills, it is developed through practice, so keep an eye out for messages you receive that deal with negative information or that attempt to persuade you to do something you're likely to resist, and analyze these messages to see how they've managed or failed to establish common ground. Mastering this concept will greatly improve the effectiveness of your writing.

SUZANNE R. ROY

OTHER THINGS YOU SHOULD KNOW

Inherent order

When applying the other Key Concepts, it is important to keep in mind the inherent order of the ideas you are presenting. If you don't do that, you will weaken your message and risk confusing your reader.

The inherent order of ideas can relate to several factors, which include, but are not limited to, the following:

- **Chronology** – If, for example, the subject of your message is a process that occurs in time, or a series of events that are best understood in terms of a time sequence, then you will make that message clearer if you present the subject chronologically – i.e., if you organize the parts in a recognizable sequence that goes from past to present to future (or vice versa) or if you use transitional terms to assist the reader in recognizing the inherent order of the ideas being presented.

- **Spatial composition** – If the subject of your message exists in space – for example, a piece of equipment – and you are trying to identify or explain its parts, your message will be most clear if you make it possible for your reader to see how the parts relate to each other in space by maintaining an order that allows readers to visualize what you are saying without having to struggle to piece your message together themselves. This is like providing a picture with a jigsaw puzzle rather than simply presenting the individual puzzle pieces in a jumble that requires guess work to assemble.

- **Logic** – If the subject of your message involves parts or processes that are connected by ideas – e.g., by the concepts of cause and effect or induction and deduction – you will be most effective if you build logical order into your message through the use of logical transition terms and sequences.

- **Degree of importance** – If the subject of your message involves parts that vary in importance, you will do well to organize them with that in mind, remembering that first and last positions are the positions of greatest emphasis. It is normally wisest to build to the most important ideas rather than to begin with the most important or to bury the most important in the middle of your message.

- **Climactic impact** – If the subject of your message involves surprise or suspense, you will have the most effect on your reader if you build from the least dramatic element to the most dramatic, leaving wrap-up information for the end as concluding material after the climax to help end the message on a calm note.

Example of inherent order:

Here's a sentence that illustrates the concept:

When was the last time you verified that your home network was secure, or changed your passwords?

In that sentence, the writer has moved from a broad concept (verifying the security of a network) to a narrow concept (changing passwords). There are two factors at work here that suggest that the ideas should have been presented in reverse order:

- From a persuasion standpoint, the first item encountered should be the easiest to accomplish and the most familiar to the reader.

- The last item is normally more important and, therefore, worthy of being emphasized by being mentioned last.

Since the reader should find it easier to change passwords than to verify the security of the network, that concept should be presented first. Since verifying the security of the network is a critical piece of advice, it should be mentioned last so that it is not forgotten when the reader moves away from the message to perform the easiest task.

Suggested revision:

> *When was the last time you changed your passwords or verified that your home Wi-Fi network was secure?*

To revise your writing for inherent order, I recommend the following 5-step revision process:

Step 1: Scan the message **and list** the items being discussed in the order presented.

Step 2: Analyze the message more closely to determine its subject and purpose, and identify what you believe to be the inherent order of the major ideas being presented.

Step 3: Compare the two lists to determine whether or not the major ideas were presented in the best order.

Step 4: Plan the revision based on the determination you've made.

Step 5: Revise the text, if necessary.

Exercise:

Here's part of a message written for use on a bank's website:

> *If you have a high deductible health care plan, are not covered by Medicare and not claimed as a dependent, you may qualify for a Health Savings Account (HSA) to help cover qualified medical expenses.*

> *Distributions are tax free if used for qualified medical expenses.*

- *The funds in the HSA carry forward from year to year until you use them, unlike a Flexible Spending Account (FSA) where all funds must be used by the end of the year or they are lost.*

- *'Portable' in that the account will stay with you from job to job*

- *You may have either a single or a family HSA, depending on who is covered under your health care plan.*

- *For current contribution limits, please see Publication 969 at IRS.gov*

- *Contributions made by yourself may be used as a tax deduction, and you can make contributions for the previous year until April 15th (tax day).*

Step 1: The items being discussed all relate to HSAs and include the following:

- Eligibility requirements
- Tax-free qualified distributions
- The fact that unused funds carry forward
- The "portability" of the account
- The types of plans available
- The source of information about HSAs
- The tax-deductible nature of the contributions and the contribution deadline

Step 2: The subject of the message is HSA plans, and the purpose is to inform the reader about such plans. The major ideas appear to involve four types of information that should be presented in a logical order based on how the reader might find them most meaningful:

- Eligibility requirements would come first, since non-eligible individuals would probably be wasting their time reading about plans to which they could not subscribe.

- Basic plan features would come next, since eligible individuals would want to know about the plans before deciding on a specific plan to look into. The features themselves should be presented chronologically in terms of when they might be used by the reader.

- The types of plans available would follow, for those individuals who are eligible and interested in the basic features of HSAs.

- Information resources would be mentioned last, for readers who need more details. To mention these resources at the beginning might cause readers to turn to the resources before reading the writer's message.

Step 3: In comparing the two lists, you should have noted the following:

- ➢ Some of the ideas in your first list are out of order.

Step 4: You now know know that:

☑ You must reorganize some of the ideas based on logical and chronological order.

Step 5: Let's compare the original message with one possible revision:

<u>Original version</u>

If you have a high deductible health care plan, are not covered by Medicare and not claimed as a dependent, you may qualify for a Health Savings Account (HSA) to help cover qualified medical expenses.

Distributions are tax free if used for qualified medical expenses.

- *The funds in the HSA carry forward from year to year until you use them, unlike a Flexible Spending Account (FSA) where all funds must be used by the end of the year or they are lost.*

- *'Portable' in that the account will stay with you from job to job*

- *You may have either a single or a family HSA, depending on who is covered under your health care plan.*

- *For current contribution limits, please see Publication 969 at IRS.gov*

- *Contributions made by yourself may be used as a tax deduction, and you can make contributions for the previous year until April 15th (tax day).*

<u>Revised version</u>

If you have a high deductible health care plan, are not covered by Medicare, and are not claimed as a dependent by anyone, you may qualify for a Health Savings Account (HAS) to help cover qualified medical expenses.

- *HSA contributions are tax deductible and may be made until April 15th (tax day) of the next tax year.*

- *HSA funds carry forward from year to year until you use them, unlike Flexible Spending Account (FSA) funds, which are lost if you don't use them by the end of the year.*

- *Distributions (i.e., withdrawals) from a HSA are tax free if used for qualified medical expenses.*

- *The HSA account is "portable," so it will stay with you from job to job.*

You may choose either a single or a family HSA, depending on who is covered under your health care plan. For more information and current contribution limits, please see Publication 969 at IRS.gov.

<u>Please note that we've stuck to the inherent order (logical and chronological) described in your 2nd list.</u>

- ✪ Eligibility (first paragraph) is followed by a bulleted list of features.

✪ Those features begin with the most important issues for most people – the tax deductibility of the plan and the deadline for making a contribution, followed by the plan's "carry forward" feature, the distribution information, and the plan's "portability." This order is logical and also chronological, since contributions must be made before the other features kick in, and since, in many instances, the annual carrying forward would occur before any distributions were taken, and the portability might not come into play before a first distribution is made.

✪ The message ends by mentioning the types of plans available and the reference to a resource for further information.

Transitions

The use of transitional words or phrases can help you to make the inherent order of your ideas obvious to your reader. Here are some examples of those words and phrases:

- Chronological terms: at first, then, next, later...

- Spatial terms: on the right, here, farther back...

- Climactic: first, more importantly, most importantly

Transitional words and phrases can also be used to establish how ideas are related to each other. For example:

- Sequential terms: first, second, third, last of all...

- Contrast terms: in contrast, to the contrary, however...
- Logical terms: as a result, consequently, therefore...

NOTE: Transitional words and phrases are useful and necessary but should not be overused because they are mechanical ways of establishing coherence and they call attention to themselves. Rely on the inherent order of ideas as much as possible to achieve coherence in your writing.

Taking the right approach

In determining which Key Concepts to use, you must know your subject, your purpose, and your reader. When approaching the revision process, keep the following in mind as you determine the type of information you are dealing with:

- If you are dealing with <u>good</u> or <u>neutral</u> information, you must be clear and get to the point quickly. Emphasis techniques (KC #1) can be particularly useful here.

- If you are dealing with <u>negative</u> information, you must begin and end with neutral or positive comments and be careful not to link the reader to the negative information unless it's necessary for the reader's safety or well-being. Personalization (KC #2), Positive & Negative (KC #4), and Common Ground (KC #5) can be especially helpful with this type of message.

☞ If you are trying to be <u>persuasive</u> or are dealing with sales information, you must focus on the reader's needs and you must usually end with a specific call for reader action. Personalization (KC #2), Features and Benefits (KC #3), and Common Ground (KC #5) can be very helpful with this type of message.

☞ If you are writing a <u>formal</u> report, you will usually be expected to present the ideas clearly, objectively, and dispassionately. Emphasis techniques (KC #1) and Personalization (KC #2, with a focus on the impersonal) should help you to write effectively.

CONCLUSION

Remember that all of the Key Concepts should be used to enhance and render more effective the message you are trying to get across.

- This requires that you know exactly what you are trying to say and how you want your reader to react to that message.

- It also requires that you know your reader and how he/she is likely to react to the type of message you are sending.

If used properly, the Key Concepts discussed in this book should provide you with an objective means of revising your correspondence so that your message is presented clearly and effectively and in a form suited to the specific reader you are addressing.

ABOUT THE AUTHOR

Suzanne R. Roy earned her Master's Degree in English from the University of Maine in Orono and taught basic and business writing for several years in the University of Maine system. She is currently a self-employed business consultant and uses her writing and editing skills on a regular basis.

REVISING FOR EFFECT is the second text she has published that deals with the writing process. The first, *Understanding CLAUSE AND EFFECT,* deals with the impact of clause recognition on the development of effective editing skills.

www.ingramcontent.com/pod-product-compliance
Lightning Source LLC
Chambersburg PA
CBHW070115290526
45789CB00005B/2031